D0510706

success

Pre-Intermediate
Students' Book

Stuart McKinlay
Bob Hastings

PEARSON
Longman

Reading	Listening	Speaking	Writing
	Personal interviews Conversation with an old friend	Interviewing a partner about habits and changes in life	
Newspaper article about British identity	People talking about their identity	Ranking things that are most important for your identity	
Famous quotations A post on a message board			A personal introduction
	Dialogues: people with different opinions	Sounding interested Roleplay	
	Dialogues: a couple on holiday/talking about holiday plans	Talking about plans for the near future Planning a holiday	
An article about a charity walk	Following an itinerary	Planning a fundraising walk	
Adverts for working holidays	Speakers talking about plans A phone call making enquiries	Talking about your country Asking for information	
Emails asking for information		Describing a photo	**Writing skills:** Formal emails
A piece of personal writing about the first day at school	People talking about their first day at secondary school	Describing a photo Pronunciation (Past Simple)	A personal anecdote
An article about dyslexia		Talking about abilities	
A questionnaire about childhood	A personal anecdote A reunion party	Talking about past habits Meeting people in ten years	
		Asking for/giving permission	
Anecdotes: Eureka moments	Guessing the context from audio clues	Talking about what you were doing at a specific time	
A quiz about sleep A magazine article about sleep		Describing a photo	
	Stories of memorable days Coleridge and *Kubla Khan*	Recounting a past event	
An anecdote: The invention of TV			**Writing skills:** Past events
A magazine article about competing neighbours		Talking about where you live/location	
An informal email	Being shown around a house		
Two newspaper articles on modern homes	Someone describing a favourite room	Talking about household gadgets	A description of a room
	Someone describing a picture	Describing a picture	
An article on healthy eating	People talking about the kind of food they buy	Interviewing each other about eating habits	
An article on vegetarianism	People talking about diets		
	Eating out: guessing the context	Pronunciation: Word stress Complaining and apologising	
			Writing skills: Questionnaires
	Listening to a fortune teller		
An article about the future of technology		Talking about probability Talking about life in the future	
Election leaflets			An election campaign leaflet
	A radio discussion on the life of Nostradamus	Describing a photo Talking about the future	

Reading	Listening	Speaking	Writing
A personality test	A phone conversation Interviews about work		
An article about unusual jobs			
A formal letter	Phone calls and messages	Roleplay: Taking and leaving phone messages	
A CV and a job application form	A job interview	Being interviewed for a job	**Writing skills:** Application forms
	A family argument A phone call	Asking and talking about things you have experienced	
An interview about a 50th wedding anniversary	People talking about their relationships with others	Describing a photo Talking about relationships	
A short story about a family	Song: *Ain't no sunshine*		
Text messages A couple gossiping	A discussion about piercings	Describing a photo; Expressing opinions; Relationships	A text message
A quiz about the media Extracts from newspapers			
An article about TV		A class survey on TV viewing	
	Extracts from the radio A radio phone-in	Explaining, repeating, interrupting and hesitating	
A letter to a newspaper Phrases for formal letter-writing	An Internet message		**Writing skills:** Formal letter (1)
Anecdotes about crimes	An unsuccessful crime		
A newspaper report on a crime	A dramatised detective story	A murder mystery	
A story about a criminal			
An advert for a lost item	A conversation with a friend about a problem	Expressing fear, shock and surprise; giving reassurance	An advert
Film reviews A poem			
A programme for an arts festival	A conversation about which events to go to	Making and responding to suggestions	A film review
An article about graffiti		A debate about art	
An informal email Short messages/notes			**Writing skills:** Short notes/messages
	Two interviews with people about sport	Talking about sports you would like to try	
An article about a teenage explorer			
An advert for a medicine	A conversation about health Short dialogues about health		A list of rules Giving advice
A 'get well soon' email	A conversation at the doctor's surgery A radio phone-in	Asking for and giving advice	
A quiz on a website	Two people trying a quiz	Using question tags	
An article about Europe	Giving opinions on the EU		
	A radio arts programme People talking about ambitions	Talking about wishes, plans and intentions	
A letter giving information		Discussing your country	**Writing skills:** A formal letter (2)

CD 1.1 Texts recorded on Class CD/Cassette   CD ROM Texts recorded on CD ROM

5

Who am I?

Read, listen and talk about identity.
Practise the Present Simple and Present Continuous; state/action verbs; personality adjectives.
Focus on expressing interest; reading for the main ideas.
Write a personal introduction.

GRAMMAR AND LISTENING

1 Look at the photo. What can you say about this person just by looking at the photo?

- How old is he?
- Where does he come from?
- Anything else about him?

2 〔CD 1.2〕 Read what Patrick's friends and family say about him. Match the texts 1–6 below with the speakers. Then listen and check.

sister	☐	friend	☐
mother	☐	band member	☐
father	☐	girlfriend	☐

1 We both belong to a rock band. Paddy is the drummer. Listen! He's playing the drums now. We're doing really well these days – we're getting quite popular.

2 It's funny, we never call him Patrick. He's just Paddy to us. Unfortunately, I don't see him very much now but w~~e~~ often email each other. We're really interested in footba~~ll~~.

3 I come from Ireland and my wife's English – I think Paddy's very proud to have some Irish blood in him!

4 Paddy's five years older than me. He hates the music I listen to and he doesn't like my friends, but he's OK.

5 I'm really proud of Patrick. He comes home to visit us quite often. In fact, he's staying here at the moment because it's the Christmas holidays.

6 He's studying at London University. I love him but he's very busy. He belongs to lots of different clubs and societies, but he's always late.

3 **CD 1.2** Listen again and answer the questions.

1 What is the name of Patrick's band?
2 Which football team does he support?
3 What is his nationality?
4 How old is he?
5 Where do his parents live?
6 What is he studying?
7 Which club does he belong to?

4 **What kind of person is Patrick? Which words do NOT describe him?**

lazy   clever   talkative   romantic   punctual
quiet   pessimistic   musical   cheerful

5 Were any of your predictions to Exercise 1 correct?

Work it out

6 Match statements 1–5 with definitions a–e.

1 We often email each other. ☐
2 He's staying with us at the moment. ☐
3 We're getting quite popular these days. ☐
4 I come from Ireland. ☐
5 Listen! He's playing the drums now. ☐

a a fact that doesn't change
b a routine or a habit
c something that's temporary
d something that's changing
e something that's happening now

7 Look at the texts in Exercise 2. Which tenses are used with these time expressions?

never   often   these days   now   always
at the moment

Check it out

Present Simple and Present Continuous

We use the Present Simple for routines/habits and facts that don't change.

We often email each other.   I come from Ireland.

Time expressions: never, often, sometimes, usually, regularly, always

We use the Present Continuous for things happening now, temporary situations and change and development.

He's playing the drums now.   He's staying with us at the moment.
We're getting quite popular these days.

Time expressions: at the moment, these days, now, this term/year

8 Circle the correct words.

1 He *isn't watching / doesn't watch* a match now. He's in the library.
2 Paddy *often watches / is often watching* football matches with his friends.
3 *Do you work / Are you working* or can I come in?
4 My English *is getting / gets* a lot better.
5 He usually *stays / is staying* in his flat in London, but he *is staying / stays* with his parents at the moment.
6 I *spend / am spending* more time with my girlfriend these days.
7 We *don't write / aren't writing* to each other very often.

9 **CD 1.3** Listen to what is happening in Paddy's life these days. Complete the sentences with a verb.

1 Paddy _____ to bed very late at the moment.
2 He _____ more time with the band.
3 He _____ much time with his girlfriend.
4 He _____ very well at the moment.

10 What is happening in your life at the moment? Tell your partner.

I'm ... at the moment. I'm also ... these days.

11 **CD 1.4** Listen and answer the questions.

1 What music does Paddy usually listen to?
2 What music is he listening to at the moment?
3 What kind of books does Paddy usually read?
4 What is he reading at the moment?

12 In pairs, ask and answer questions about your interests.

science fiction   crime   fantasy   horror
short stories   detective stories   classic

classical   jazz   techno   hip-hop   reggae
rock   soul   pop   heavy metal

	You	Your partner
1 What sort of music do you usually listen to?	I usually listen to	Robert likes ... .
2 What bands do you like?		
3 What sort of books do you enjoy?		
4 What are you reading at the moment?		

READING AND SPEAKING

1 Look at the map and complete the text.

Great Britain is an island with three different nations: [1]_____, Scotland and [2]_____ . Many learners of English say *England* or *English* when they mean *Britain* or *British*. This is a mistake! The United Kingdom (UK) is a political name for England, [3]_____ , Wales and Northern Ireland together. When people say *Britain* or *British*, they are talking about the UK too.

2 Read the article on page 9 quickly and decide what the main idea of the article is. Don't worry about new words.

1 Languages in Britain ☐
2 Multicultural Britain ☐
3 Britain's crisis ☐

3 〔CD ROM〕 Quickly read the article again. Circle the words in each paragraph that show the main ideas.

4 Use your circled words to help you match the headings with the paragraphs. There are two headings you don't need.

1 Religion and language ☐
2 Different generations ☐
3 Statistics ☐
4 Geography and population ☐
5 Entertainment and food ☐

5 Look back at Exercises 2–4 and circle the correct words in Train Your Brain.

TRAIN YOUR BRAIN | Reading skills

Understanding the main ideas

When you want to understand the main ideas in a text:

a *Don't worry about / Check* any words you don't know.
b As you read, decide what the main ideas of each *sentence / paragraph* are.
c *Memorise / Circle* a few words or phrases to help you remember the main ideas.

---

6 In pairs, decide which sentence is the best summary of the article.

1 A typical British person doesn't know what his/her nationality is.
2 Many people don't want to call themselves British.
3 Britain's identity is changing and this makes life in Britain more exciting.

7 Look at the underlined words in the text and match them with the definitions.

1 a belief in a god or gods
2 to be able to speak two languages
3 people who live in the same area or town
4 the number of people living in a country
5 having many types of people or things at the same time
6 having people from many different cultures

8 〔CD 1.5〕 Listen to people talking about their identity. Match speakers 1–5 with opinions a–e.

1 Iman ☐
2 Steve ☐
3 Adil ☐
4 Megan ☐
5 Robert ☐

a My home town is very important but I also feel European.
b My nationality is very important – I always support the national team.
c The language that I speak at home is very important to me.
d My religion is very important to me.
e I'm British but I usually say I'm a citizen of the world.

9 Look at the ideas below. Which three are the most important to your identity?

citizen of the world
club/sports team
family and friends
European, Asian, American
community and home town
nationality **school**
religion **language**

10 Talk about your choices in Exercise 9 with the rest of the class.

A For me, nationality is very important because I love my country.
B I don't agree – nationality isn't important – family and friends are really important.

Has Britain got an identity crisis?

Now that the United Kingdom's latest population statistics are available, Terry Bleater asks, 'Do the British know who they are?'

A To the rest of the world, people from the UK are British. But it's surprising to learn that only 31 percent of people in the UK say they are just British. In fact, nearly half the <u>population</u> say their nationality is something else – English, Scottish, Welsh, Irish or perhaps Vietnamese, Indian or Somali. Some people, about 16 percent, even say that they have two nationalities: they are British, but also Scottish or Chinese. There are hundreds of possibilities! Are we confused? Is it a problem?

B No, it doesn't seem to be. Britain is changing all the time and we are not just tolerant of differences – we are proud of them. We enjoy the diversity that <u>multiculturalism</u> gives us. The ethnic groups that exist in the UK bring with them at least six major <u>religions</u>, including Christianity, Islam, Hinduism, Buddhism, Sikhism and Judaism. Each <u>community</u> contributes its own culture and language. Britain still has two official languages; English and Welsh, but we speak many more – approximately 150 in fact – from Mandarin Chinese to Urdu. Many of us are even <u>bilingual</u>.

C And then there's the fun stuff that <u>cultural diversity</u> brings, in music, food and the arts. The days of fish and chips are behind us, as a walk around the capital shows. Almost every district has Lebanese, Chinese, Thai and Vietnamese restaurants. Thousands of Londoners visit the Notting Hill Carnival every year to dance to steel bands, reggae, soca, calypso and jazz. Our cinemas show films from India and South America and thousands of people fill our pubs and clubs to listen to everything from Irish dance bands to African hip-hop. Welcome to New Britain: a confident, tolerant country which is proud of its many cultures.

VOCABULARY

1 **Think Back!** Complete the personality adjectives that describe Paddy.

1 ch _ _ _ _ _ l	2 c _ _ v _ _
3 h _ _ _ - w _ _ _ _ _	4 m _ _ _ _ t
5 p _ _ si _ i _ _ i _	6 r _ m _ _ _ _ _

7 t _ _ k _ _ _ v _

2 Underline personality adjectives that have a positive meaning. Use a dictionary if you need to.

stupid	rude
tolerant	optimistic
lazy	friendly
jealous	proud
arrogant	selfish
bossy	boring
quiet	polite
shy	helpful
lively	confident
generous	

3 Match adjectives 1–6 with their opposite meanings a–f.

1 stupid ☐   **a** modest
2 lazy ☐   **b** talkative
3 arrogant ☐   **c** boring
4 quiet ☐   **d** polite
5 lively ☐   **e** hard-working
6 rude ☐   **f** clever

4 Choose the correct answer.

1 Jessica is a very _____ girl. She loves meeting new people.
   a generous   **b** selfish   **c** friendly
2 The British are quite _____ . They feel uncomfortable with strangers.
   a confident   **b** cheerful   **c** shy
3 Tom is extremely _____ . He thinks he's better than everyone else.
   a arrogant   **b** tolerant   **c** helpful
4 My brother is always _____ . He's very positive about the future.
   a jealous   **b** optimistic   **c** serious
5 Dan is very _____ . He always has a smile on his face!
   a cheerful   **b** ambitious   **c** tolerant
6 Anna's a _____ person. She always tells other people what to do.
   a lively   **b** talkative   **c** bossy

5 Work in pairs and follow the instructions.

- Choose five adjectives that describe your personality and two that don't.
- Tell your partner what your adjectives are. He/She guesses which two do NOT describe you.

GRAMMAR AND WRITING

1 **CD 1.6** Read the quotations. Write the missing verbs. Then listen and check.

agree   hate   understand   want (x 2)

1 I hear and I forget. I see and I remember. I do and I _____ .
Confucius

2 Whenever people _____ with me, I always think I must be wrong.
Oscar Wilde

3 It's not that I'm afraid to die. I just don't _____ to be there when it happens!
Woody Allen

4 I'm not a vegetarian because I love animals. I'm a vegetarian because I _____ plants.
A. Whitney Brown

5 I _____ to be alone.
Greta Garbo

Work it out

2 Look at these examples and answer the questions.

I often go home at lunchtime.
I want to be alone.

1 Which verb describes:
 a an action? _____
 b a state (thoughts, feelings, beliefs)? _____
2 Which of these verbs can you use in the Present Continuous?
3 Look at the quotations in Exercise 1 again. Which verbs describe states?

Check it out

State and action verbs

We use simple and continuous tenses with action verbs. The meaning of the verb doesn't change.

I often **eat** fruit. → **I'm eating** an apple now.
I **go** home at lunchtime. → **I'm going** home now.

We can only use simple tenses with state verbs (e.g. believe, belong, hate, know, like, love, need, prefer, see, understand).

I **want** to be alone.	NOT	I'm wanting to be alone.
Yes, I **remember** now.	NOT	I'm remembering now.

3 Tick the correct sentences and correct the wrong ones.

1 Jack isn't liking the book. ☐
2 I'm listening to a great piece of music. ☐
3 George doesn't know the answer. ☐
4 I'm sorry but I'm not agreeing with you. ☐
5 I'm thinking my answer is wrong. ☐
6 You aren't understanding the joke. ☐

4 Complete Michel's message to the *English Contacts* website with the verbs below.

understand love belong like want think

◁ Back ▷ Forward ✕ Stop ↻ Refresh ⌂ Home AutoFill Print ✉ Mail

Address: @ www1.englishcontacts.com

Favorites | History | Search | Scrapbook | Page Holder

English Contacts

Posted by Michel at 14.37

My name's Michel and I'm twenty-two. I come from Belgium but at the moment I'm studying English in London. I ¹_____ painting and I ²_____ to be a professional artist in the future. I also ³_____ to a youth theatre group in Liège and I enjoy acting. I don't have time for sport at the moment but I like swimming. I also ⁴_____ crime novels (at the moment I'm reading books by P.D. James). Thanks to my course, I ⁵_____ my English is getting better and now I ⁶_____ more when people speak to me. My friends say that I'm romantic and cheerful. Oh, I'm also crazy about football. This is my first post – if you have the same interests as me, please write! My email address is michel@webmail.be

Posted by Murat at 19.27

Hi Michel,
First of all, welcome to English Contacts! I am also living in London at the moment and studying at a language school in Camden. I come from Istanbul in Turkey and I enjoy Art too. In fact I want to work as an artist in London when I finish my studies.

5 Read Michel's message again. Tick the things he writes about.

Age ☐
Nationality ☐
Where he lives ☐
Family ☐
How well he knows English ☐
Hobbies, interests, sports ☐
Personality ☐

6 Now write a short introduction about yourself for the *English Contacts* website. Write about the things in Exercise 5.

LISTENING AND SPEAKING

1 Look at the photo and answer the questions.

- What is the man's job?
- What kind of person do you need to be to do this job?

2 CD 1.7 Listen and answer the questions.

1 Why does Mr Jordan want to speak to Jay?
2 Why do customers complain about Jay? Give two reasons.
3 Where do Jay and Mr Jordan work?
4 What's the relationship between Jay and Mr Jordan?

3 CD 1.7 Listen again. Tick true and cross false.

1 Jay is often late for work. ☐
2 Jay is working every evening this week. ☐
3 Jay serves the customers very quickly. ☐
4 *Jordan's* is a quiet restaurant. ☐
5 Jay is becoming careless at work. ☐
6 Jay is falling asleep at work. ☐
7 Mr Jordan wants Jay to stay in his job. ☐

4 What kind of person is Jay? In pairs, write down three adjectives. Then compare your ideas with another pair.

1 _____
2 _____
3 _____

5 In pairs, answer the questions.

1 Why do you think Jay is having problems at work?
2 Why does he need the money?

A I think Jay is having problems because he's lazy.
B No, I don't think he's lazy. I think he just doesn't like his job.

6 CD 1.8 Listen to Jay's conversation with his friend Nick. Were your answers to Exercise 5 correct?

7 Work in pairs. Write three more adjectives to describe Jay and compare them with your answers to Exercise 4. Do you have a different opinion of him now?

1 _____
2 _____
3 _____

8 In pairs, complete the conversation between Nick and Mr Jordan. Practise saying your dialogue, then perform it for the class.

Student A
You are Mr Jordan, Jay's boss at the restaurant. You are very unhappy with Jay because you are having problems with him at work.

Student B
You are Nick, Jay's best friend and Mr Jordan's neighbour. You think that Jay is a wonderful guy – hard-working, intelligent and helpful. You also know that Jay is working very hard to save money to train to be a pilot in the Flying Doctor Service.

Mr Jordan	So, you know Jay?
Nick	Oh yes, I know him very well. He's my best friend actually.
Mr Jordan	Jay is working at my restaurant. I'm having problems with him. He _____ .
Nick	That's surprising. I think Jay's _____ .
Mr Jordan	Well, he's not a very good waiter. He has to look for another job!
Nick	Really? But, Mr Jordan, Jay really needs the money. He _____ .
Mr Jordan	A pilot in the Flying Doctor Service? Perhaps I should give him another chance.

SPEAKING

1 [CD 1.9] Listen to the two dialogues. What's the difference between them?

2 [CD 1.9] Study **Speak Out**. Listen to the second dialogue again and complete it with expressions from **Speak Out**. Then, in pairs, practise the dialogue.

Sarah What do you do, Rob?
Rob I work for a TV company.
Sarah Oh ¹_____? ²_____!
Rob Yes, it's great fun. So, … what about you? What do you do?
Sarah Well, I work for a fashion magazine.
Rob ³_____? ⁴_____! Where?
Sarah It's in central London – St Martin's Lane.
Rob ⁵_____? ⁶_____! Let's meet up.

SPEAK OUT | Expressing interest

Echo questions		Other expressions
Have you?	Has he?	Really?
Do you?	Does she?	Brilliant!/Great!/Wow!/Cool!
Can you?	Can he?	How interesting!
Are you?	Is she?	What an interesting thing to do!
Is it?	Are there?	That sounds brilliant/great/cool/good/interesting!
		That's brilliant/great/cool/good/interesting!

---

3 [CD 1.10] Match sentences 1–6 with echo questions a–f. Listen and check. In pairs, practise saying the echo questions.

1 I've got three sisters. ☐
2 I come from Lisbon. ☐
3 My sister can speak Italian. ☐
4 I'm bilingual. ☐
5 Seville is very beautiful. ☐
6 There are some very old buildings in my home town. ☐

a Are you?
b Is it?
c Have you?
d Do you?
e Are there?
f Can she?

4 [CD 1.11] Listen to the sentences. Answer with the correct echo question. Then listen and check.

1 My mum's a vegetarian.
  Is she?
2 I come from London but I live in Berlin.
3 There are two official languages in my country.
4 French is my mother tongue.
5 My brother can do karate.
6 I've got my own website.

5 Complete sentences 1–5 with information about yourself. Then work in pairs and make dialogues. Take turns.

Student A
1 I've got _____ .
2 My parents come from _____ .
3 I'm getting much better at _____ these days.
4 I can _____ .
5 There's a fantastic new _____ in town.

A I've got some new CDs.
B Have you? / Really?

6 Write six questions to ask your partner. Use the prompts below.

Do you like … ?
Are you interested in … ?
Have you got … ?
Can you … ?
What are you doing on … ?
Are you getting better at … ?
Do you belong to … ?

7 Work in pairs. Ask each other your questions from Exercise 6. Remember to sound interested!

A Are you interested in history?
B Yes, very much.
A Oh, are you?

8 Look at the cartoon and complete the caption with the correct echo question.

'She also plays the violin in the National Philharmonic Orchestra, you know.'

Globetrotter!

Read, listen and talk about future plans and travel.
Practise the Present Continuous and *going to* for future plans and intentions; travel vocabulary.
Focus on asking for information.
Write formal and informal emails.

GRAMMAR AND SPEAKING

1 Read and answer the questions.

- Do you enjoy travelling?
- Which countries interest you most? Why? Tell the class.

2 Look at the pictures and read the postcard below. Which countries do the couple finally decide to visit?

3 **CD 1.12** Listen to the conversation. Is the holiday a success? Why?/Why not?

'We need a holiday!'

'We're so excited! We're going to visit Europe this summer.'

Travel

'How about somewhere different – Hawaii or Europe?'
'Europe sounds good!'

'Sorry, I can't talk now. We're flying to London in four hours.'

Hi George,   25th August

Well, here we are in London. We're visiting Buckingham Palace and Big Ben this afternoon.

Then after lunch we're taking a coach to Windsor Castle. Tomorrow morning we're flying to Paris and then on Thursday we're staying the night in Amsterdam.

We're planning to be in Italy on Saturday morning.

Then we're

George Laval
2707 Elk Way
Toronto
Ontario
Canada

Work it out

4 Look at the underlined sentences in the pictures and answer the questions.

Which sentence talks about:
a a definite plan for the near future?
b an unfinalised plan, future intention or ambition?

Check it out

Future arrangements and intentions

We use *going to* to talk about future intentions, ambitions, or unfinalised plans.

We're going to visit Europe this summer.
I'm going to study Economics at university.

We use the Present Continuous to talk about a definite plan in the near future. We usually mention the time and/or place as well.

We're flying to London in four hours.
We're visiting Buckingham Palace this afternoon.

5 Choose the best response to situations 1–5.

1 You meet a friend at the station. He's running to the platform and holding his ticket. He says:
a I'm going to catch the train to London.
b I'm catching the train to London.

2 Your ferry is delayed for six hours! You're very angry. You say:
a I'm going to write a letter of complaint.
b I'm writing a letter of complaint.

3 Your friend asks you to babysit this evening. You can't help. You say:
a I'm meeting my friends at the swimming pool at eight.
b I'm going to meet my friends at the swimming pool at eight.

4 A friend is coming out of the travel agent's with a lot of holiday brochures. You ask where he wants to go on holiday. He says:
a I think I'm going to visit Scandinavia this year.
b I think I'm visiting Scandinavia this year.

5 Your friends are packing a tent into the back of their car. They say:
a We're going camping.
b We're going to go camping.

Mind the trap!

With verbs that describe leisure activities (*hike, swim, sail, camp, sightsee*) you usually add the verb *go* + verb + *-ing*

I'm **going** fish**ing** tomorrow. NOT ~~I'm fishing~~ tomorrow.

6 (CD 1.13) Complete the conversation. Use the Present Continuous or *going to* and the verbs in brackets. Then listen and check.

Tom Hi Louise!
Louise Oh, hi Tom! How are things?
Tom We're just packing our suitcases. We ¹_____ (leave) for the airport in a few minutes.
Louise Where ²_____ (you/go)?
Tom We ³_____ (go) to Poland for a week. We ⁴_____ (fly) to Cracow at midday.
Louise So are you staying in Cracow all week?
Tom No, we ⁵_____ (stay) in Cracow for three nights. We've got a reservation in a really nice guest house in the city centre. Then we ⁶_____ (hike) in the Tatra mountains for a few days. Well, we're not sure yet – it depends on the weather!
Louise Lucky you! Adam and I think we ⁷_____ (spend) a week or two in Turkey, maybe in August.

7 In pairs, read the adverts below. Choose a holiday and discuss your plans.

Discuss:
• where you plan to go.
• how you're going to get there.
• when you're leaving and where from.
• where you're going to stay.
• what you plan to do when you arrive.

European Holidays

Fly to Greece this summer and experience a superb camping holiday on a Greek island. Ideal for swimming, sunbathing and snorkelling!

Depart 2 June from New York to Athens, Greece Return 2 July

On Your Bike!
Extraordinary cycling holidays in The Netherlands

Accommodation in local youth hostels
Sightseeing tours in Leiden and Utrecht

Coach from London to Amsterdam 2 May Amsterdam to London 9 May

8 In pairs, ask about your future plans. Use the Present Continuous, *going to* and the times below.

tonight   this weekend   next summer

A What are you doing this weekend?
B On Saturday evening I'm meeting a friend. I think I'm going to play squash on Sunday morning.

READING AND LISTENING

1 Before you read the text, answer the questions.

- What does *charity* mean to you?
- How many different types of charity can you think of?
- Do you know anyone who collects money for charity?

2 Quickly read the article and answer the questions. Don't worry about new words.

1 Jamie is going to the Himalayas
  a for a holiday.
  b to do something exciting and help people too.
2 Jamie's lecturers
  a are helping him to raise money.
  b are also travelling to Nepal.
3 Jamie is busy before the trip because
  a he needs to be very fit.
  b he has important university exams.

3 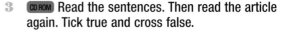 Read the sentences. Then read the article again. Tick true and cross false.

1 Jamie is older than his sister. ☐
2 This is Jamie's first holiday abroad. ☐
3 Jamie is studying Sociology at university. ☐
4 Jamie is planning to raise £5,000 after his trip to Nepal. ☐
5 Jamie is planning to give all the money to charity. ☐
6 Jamie goes running every evening. ☐
7 Jackie doesn't want Jamie to go on the trip. ☐

4 In pairs, match words 1–5 with the definitions a–e.

1 trek (n) [para. 1] ☐
2 raise money (v) [para. 1] ☐
3 disabled (adj) [para. 1] ☐
4 charity (n) [para. 2] ☐
5 challenge (n) [para 6] ☐

a describing somebody who cannot use a part of their body
b a long, difficult journey on foot
c something that tests your skills or abilities
d an organisation that helps people who are poor or sick
e to collect money that you can use to help people

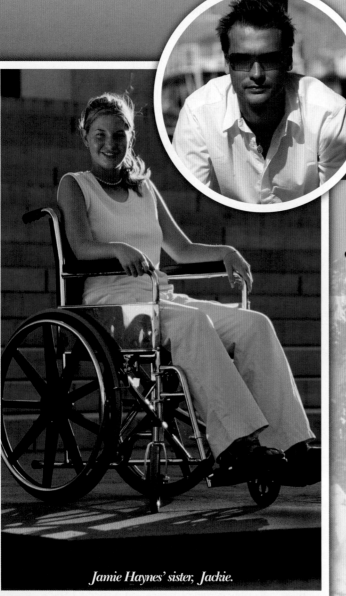

Jamie Haynes' sister, Jackie.

Jamie's
Charity Challenge

Edinburgh student, Jamie Haynes, is planning to achieve his lifetime ambition.

Next month he's flying to Nepal with five friends to begin a three-week trek of the Himalayas. Jamie, 20, is aiming to raise money for young disabled people at the same time. His younger sister, Jackie, who is paralysed and in a wheelchair, is the inspiration for Jamie's trip.

There's a charity called Go-Getters. It helps young people who are seriously ill or who are disabled, like my sister. 'I always enjoy travelling abroad, especially on unusual adventures, so it's a great way to combine a holiday with helping people,' says Jamie, a Sociology student at Edinburgh University.

5 Look at the map of Jamie's trek and find the following places.

Lukla   the Kosi River   a national park
Mt Everest Base Camp   Mt Everest

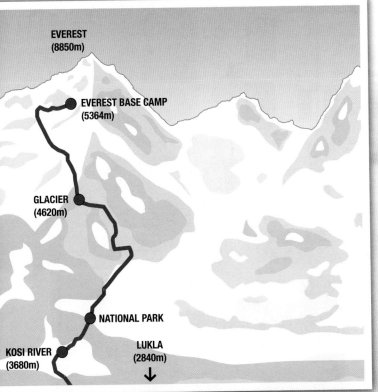

EVEREST
(8850m)

EVEREST BASE CAMP
(5364m)

GLACIER
(4620m)

NATIONAL PARK

KOSI RIVER
(3680m)

LUKLA
(2840m)

6 **CD 1.14** Listen and complete Jamie's notes about the expedition. Then listen again and check your answers.

1 Fly to Kathmandu on ___11th___ June.
2 Spend the night in a _____ .
3 Travel to Lukla on _____ June. Pick up animals there.
4 Cross the Kosi River on _____ June.
5 Spend _____ nights at the national park.
6 Camp on the glacier on _____ June.
7 Start travelling back to Kathmandu on _____ June.

7 Describe Jamie's journey. Look at the map and use the notes in Exercise 6 to help you.

Jamie's flying to Kathmandu on 11 June. Then he's ...

8 Work in groups. Imagine you are going on an expedition to raise £5,000 for charity. Decide the following things and tell the class.

- What sort of charity are you going to support? Why?
- When and where are you going?
- How are you getting there?
- Where are you going to stay?
- Do you need any special equipment?
- How are you going to raise the money before you go?

Musselburgh Gazette

Jamie is raising £5,000 before he goes. A small part of the money pays for his flight and the rest goes to Go-Getters, which organises holidays and other leisure activities for young disabled people. The charity hopes to use the money to buy a new minibus, specially designed for people in wheelchairs.

Jamie is amazed by the response of other students to his unusual idea. 'They all want to help me. It's fantastic! Next week all the other students in my group are doing a 24-hour sponsored silence. People are going to pay us to keep quiet! Some of the lecturers are going to do it as well – for some of them it's going to be very difficult!'

At the moment, Jamie is training for the trip. He goes to the gym every morning, goes running every evening and goes swimming four times a week. Jamie is also following a special high-protein diet of fish, fruit and eggs.

'We're going to walk through the high Himalayas for about seven hours every day for almost three weeks, so we need to be very fit! We're all really excited about it, but I also feel nervous. It's certainly a big challenge for all of us.'

And what does Jackie think of Jamie's plans? 'It's a great idea but a little bit crazy too! I'm so proud that Jamie and his friends want to help!' Anybody who is interested in sponsoring Jamie's trip should contact the Gazette.

LISTENING

1 Look at the photos. Match pictures 1–6 with the types of accommodation below.

campsite ☐   caravan ☐   mountain shelter ☐
youth hostel ☐   hotel ☐   guest house ☐

2 Which types of accommodation in Exercise 1 are best for these people? Why?

1 A student who wants to go backpacking. He/She doesn't have much money and wants to meet people from all over the world.
2 A couple on their honeymoon.
3 A family with a car. They want to visit as many places as possible without spending too much money.
4 Somebody who wants to relax and ski in the mountains every day.

3 [CD 1.15] Listen and match the photos in Exercise 1 with the speakers.

Jack ☐
Sam ☐
Bill ☐

4 [CD 1.15] Listen to Jack, Sam and Bill again. Match the speakers with statements 1–6.

Jack ☐ ☐   Sam ☐ ☐   Bill ☐ ☐

1 He's staying near the sea.
2 He's going backpacking.
3 He doesn't need to pay for breakfast.
4 He's travelling alone.
5 He's going to buy fresh food every day.
6 He's going to spend his holiday in the mountains.

5 [CD 1.16] Listen to Bill saying more about his holiday plans. Tick true and cross false.

1 This is Bill's first holiday in Scotland. ☐
2 Bill is starting his walk on Thursday. ☐
3 Bill is staying in Scotland for just one week. ☐
4 Bill is spending a lot of money on accommodation. ☐
5 The mountain shelters have electricity but no hot water. ☐
6 You can meet people from different countries in the shelters. ☐

6 In pairs, answer the questions.

1 Which places are popular for tourists in your country?
2 What kind of accommodation do people stay in?
3 Do you often spend your holidays in these places?

SPEAKING

1 Read the adverts for working holidays and answer the questions.

• Which holiday sounds most interesting? Why?
• Are these kinds of holiday popular in your country?

GO-GETTERS
WORKING HOLIDAY IN SCOTLAND

• Use your skills and have a great holiday at the same time!
• Work with disabled children in the beautiful Scottish highlands
• Free accommodation, food and travel
• Earn up to £150 a week
• A great chance to speak English and meet local people

Call Go-Getters now on (44) 418 672 801

❷

VOLUNTEERS NEEDED
FOR ARCHAEOLOGICAL DIG IN DORSET

• Work with students from all over the world in southwest England
• Learn about Roman Britain (we are excavating a 2,000-year-old Roman villa)
• Accommodation available, but you must pay for your ticket to the UK

Please phone (44) 242 6015901 for more information.

2 🔊 CD 1.17 Listen to the phone conversation. Which advert is this person calling about? Tick the things the student asks about.

dates ☐   food ☐
accommodation ☐   cost ☐
places available ☐

3 Study Speak Out. What do you notice about the position of the verbs after question words with indirect questions?

SPEAK OUT | Asking for information

Direct questions	Indirect questions
	Could you tell me ...
How much does it cost?	... **how much** it costs?
When does it start?	... **when** it starts?
Where is the nearest youth hostel?	... **where** the nearest youth hostel is?
What time does the train leave?	... **what time** the train leaves?
How long does the course last?	... **how long** the course lasts?
How many places are there?	... **how many** places there are?

Could you give me some information about ...
... **accommodation** (in the city)?
... **summer courses** in English?
... **entertainment** in the city?

4 🔊 CD 1.17 Listen again and look at Speak Out. Tick the questions you hear.

5 In pairs, read the advert and decide what information is missing. Compare your ideas with another pair.

FIRST CLASS
SCHOOL OF ENGLISH

Come to sunny Brighton and learn English!
✦ courses all year
✦ all levels from beginner to advanced
✦ satisfied students from all over the world!

Call us now! (44) 1788 672 801

6 You want to find out the following information. Write a direct and an indirect question for each item.

1 The start of the course
When does the course start?
Could you tell me when the course starts?
2 How many hours of classes there are a week
3 The cost of the course
4 Where you can stay

7 🔊 CD 1.18 Listen to a student calling First Class School of English. Which of your questions does he ask?

8 Work in pairs. Look at advert 1 in Exercise 1. Use Speak Out to roleplay a conversation.

Student A
You are interested in the working holiday in Scotland. You can start work on 1 August. You want to know:

• the dates of the holiday.
• where you're going to stay.
• how to get to Scotland from London.

Student B
Look at page 142.

19

VOCABULARY

1 Think Back! Write four more words in each category.

Types of accommodation	Means of transport	Holiday and leisure activities
caravan, bed and breakfast	plane, motorbike, ferry	sailing, snorkelling, fishing, cycling, sunbathing, climbing
1_____ 3_____	1_____ 3_____	1_____ 3_____
2_____ 4_____	2_____ 4_____	2_____ 4_____

2 Look at the photo below. In pairs, answer the questions.
  - What are the people doing?
  - Which country do you think the picture shows?
  - What kind of accommodation do you think they are staying in?
  - Would you like to have a holiday like this. Why?/Why not?
    Choose from these ideas.

(too) peaceful   bad/wet weather   fresh air   have fun with friends
cheap   (heavy) rucksacks   (not) exciting   relaxing
far from the city   tiring   keep fit   beautiful/dramatic scenery

  - Is this type of holiday popular in your country?
  - What sort of leisure activities are most popular in your country?

3 Circle the correct answer.

1 We've got a tent – we're going to stay *in a guest house* / *on a campsite*.
2 We're going for a *drive* / *trek* in the country in my new car!
3 We're still *loading* / *packing* our suitcases – and we're leaving in an hour!
4 I'm *booking* / *arranging* a double room at the hotel.
5 Our flight is *cancelled* / *delayed*. It's leaving later this afternoon.
6 We want to go to Bulgaria this summer. I'm going to get some *brochures* / *magazines* from the travel agent's.

4 Complete the sentences with the correct prepositions.

for   to   at   by (x 2)
on   from   in

1 Are you travelling _____ Budapest _____ coach or _____ plane?
2 We're arriving _____ Buenos Aires at midday.
3 They're walking to Kathmandu _____ foot.
4 We have to be _____ the airport at half past eleven.
5 The Moscow train departs _____ platform 3.
6 We're leaving _____ Prague tomorrow morning.

WRITING

1 **Answer the questions.**

1 Do you send emails? How often?
2 Who do you send them to?

2 **Read Gina's emails and answer the questions.**

1 Which email sounds formal and is similar to a letter? Why?
2 Which email sounds informal and is similar to a conversation? Why?

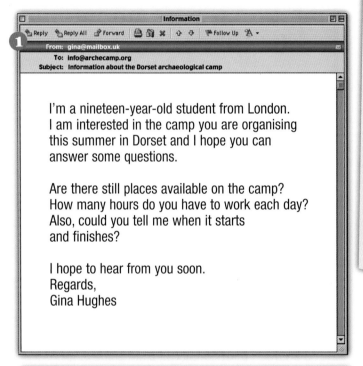

Information

From: gina@mailbox.uk
To: info@archecamp.org
Subject: Information about the Dorset archaeological camp

I'm a nineteen-year-old student from London. I am interested in the camp you are organising this summer in Dorset and I hope you can answer some questions.

Are there still places available on the camp? How many hours do you have to work each day? Also, could you tell me when it starts and finishes?

I hope to hear from you soon.
Regards,
Gina Hughes

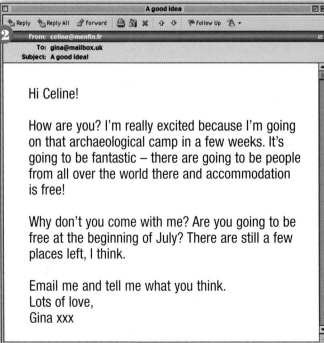

A good idea

From: celine@menfin.fr
To: gina@mailbox.uk
Subject: A good idea!

Hi Celine!

How are you? I'm really excited because I'm going on that archaeological camp in a few weeks. It's going to be fantastic – there are going to be people from all over the world there and accommodation is free!

Why don't you come with me? Are you going to be free at the beginning of July? There are still a few places left, I think.

Email me and tell me what you think.
Lots of love,
Gina xxx

3 **Match endings a–b with the emails in Exercise 2.**

a Love/Bye for now/See you/CU!
b Best wishes/Best regards/Kind regards

4 **Who do we usually send formal emails to? Tick the correct answers and say why.**

- people we don't know ☐
- institutions ☐
- friends and close family ☐
- people we know very well ☐

5 **Read Celine's email to the camp and compare it with Gina's first email in Exercise 2. Which email is better? Why?**

From	celine@menfin.fr
To	info@archecamp.org
Subject	HELP ME PLEASE!!!!!!!!!!

Hi guys

How are you? I'm Celine. I'm a fun-loving nineteen-year-old student from Nice.

My friend Gina (she's British and she's really cool) says you're doing a camp in Dorset.
I want to go too. Are there any places left or not? How much money do I need???

Write back quickly and tell me.
C U!!!!
Celine x :-D

6 **In pairs, read Train Your Brain and correct Celine's email to the camp.**

TRAIN YOUR BRAIN | Writing skills

Formal emails

a In the subject box, give a clear reason for writing your email.
b You don't need a greeting if you don't know the person's name.
c If you know the person's name, you can write *Dear* + name.
d Smileys (☺), exclamation marks (!), jokes and unimportant information aren't a good idea.
e End the email with *Best/Kind regards*.

7 **Read the advert for the First Class School of English on page 19. Write a formal email to the school.**

Find out:
- if there are still places in the Pre-Intermediate group at the moment.
- how much the course costs.
- how many students there are in the group.
- if the school can help you with accommodation.

8 **Check your partner's email. Tick each stage in Train Your Brain.**

VOCABULARY AND GRAMMAR

1 Put these words into five categories. Then add three more words from Units 1–2 to each group.

campsite   guest house   horror   hip-hop
jazz   polite   reggae   jealous
science fiction   mountain shelter
short story   snorkelling   sightseeing
tolerant   trekking

Books: _____ , _____ , _____ ,

_____ , _____ , _____

Music: _____ , _____ , _____ ,

_____ , _____ , _____

Holiday activities: _____ , _____ ,

_____ , _____ , _____ , _____

Personality adjectives: _____ , _____ ,

_____ , _____ , _____ , _____

Types of accommodation: _____ , _____ ,

_____ , _____ , _____ , _____

2 In each group circle the odd one out.

1 selfish	polite	friendly	cheerful
2 arrogant	rude	generous	bossy
3 excellent	fantastic	careless	brilliant
4 go	arrive	depart	leave
5 trek	brochure	trip	tour
6 tent	ferry	rucksack	sleeping bag

3 Complete the sentences with the correct form of the words in capital letters.

1 My brother is very _____ . He never shuts up.　　　　　　　TALK

2 Watching DVDs is my favourite form of _____ .　　　　ENTERTAIN

3 He's very _____ . He wants to be rich and famous.　　AMBITION

4 He's got a really cheerful _____ .　　　　　　　　　PERSON

5 They are collecting money for the _____ children's holidays.　ABLE

6 I had a very _____ holiday in a quiet mountain village.　　PEACE

4 Complete the second sentence so that it has a similar meaning to the first sentence. Use the word in bold and other words to complete each sentence.

1 Bill hates listening to rock music.　**like**
Bill _____ to rock music.

2 Shirley is watching TV at the moment.　**not**
Shirley _____ her homework at the moment.

3 I'm always at school on time.　**never**
I _____ for school.

4 We're going to take a train to London.　**to**
We're going to _____ train.

5 I'm going to stay at home this summer.　**not**
I'm _____ holiday this summer.

5 Complete the email. For each gap circle the correct answer.

_____
Coming to Newcastle!
🔄 Reply　🔄 Reply All　📨 Forward　🖨 📑 ✖ ⬆ ⬇　🏁 Follow Up　🅰 ▾

From: JocelynP@greatstuff.tv
To: vic172@newland.org
Subject: Coming to Newcastle!

Dear Vicky,

Thank you for your email. I ¹____ the photo! Your house looks lovely. You sound very busy at the moment. ²____ with your cousins in Cambridge or are you back home now?

I've got some news for you! I'm coming to see you during the holidays. My parents always ³____ to Scotland to see my grandparents at Easter so I can stay with you in Newcastle for a week. They ⁴____ a car this time because ours usually breaks down on long journeys – it ⁵____ very old!

At the moment I ⁶____ in the library at school. We sometimes ⁷____ an hour off to study on Tuesdays. I'm looking out of the window and unfortunately it's very grey and cloudy outside. Normally I ⁸____ basketball on Tuesday afternoon but I ⁹____ today! It's too cold.

Well, that's it. Pete and I ¹⁰____ Katy at four. We're all going to the cinema and I'm already late!

Write to me again soon. See you in Newcastle!

Love

Jocelyn
_____

1 a am loving　　**b** am going to love　　**c** love

2 a Do you still stay　　**b** Are you still staying
　c You still stay

3 a go　　**b** are going　　**c** are going to go

4 a are renting　　**b** rent　　**c** renting

5 a is getting　　**b** gets　　**c** to get

6 a am going to sit　　**b** sit　　**c** am sitting

7 a have　　**b** are having
　c are going to have

8 a play　　**b** go to play　　**c** am playing

9 a don't play　　**b** am not going to play
　c not playing

10 a to meet　　**b** meet　　**c** are meeting

PRONUNCIATION

1 ‹CD 1.19› Listen and put the words in the correct column. Then listen and check.

●●●	●●●●	●●●●	●●●●●
confident	equipment	ability	inspiration

available   citizen   community   detective
dramatic   entertainment   fantasy
biology   important   musical   population
pessimistic

LISTENING SKILLS

1 **CD 1.20** Listen. Read the sentences. Tick true and cross false.

1 Jodie is packing for a holiday. ☐
2 She's going away for a week. ☐
3 She's going to take three bags. ☐
4 Paula likes to make a list before
she packs. ☐
5 Paula tells Jodie to take two sweaters. ☐
6 Jodie's going abroad. ☐

READING SKILLS

1 Complete the text with sentences a–f. There is one extra sentence. Then, tick the best heading A–C for the text.

The importance of English as a global language is growing all the time. Of course, there are more native speakers of Chinese than of English – about a billion compared to about 400 million. ¹_____ . And this number is getting bigger every year. English is the international language of politics, business, science, transport, advertising, the media and computers. ²_____ . Even in countries like Germany, almost 90 percent of research scientists use English as their working language every day.

There are some other languages which are gaining in popularity: the number of people who speak Arabic, Chinese or Portuguese in different countries is increasing too. ³_____ . Even in the USA the fastest growing language is Spanish!

⁴_____ . There are about 6,000 languages in the world but sadly many of them have an uncertain future. In fact, about twenty languages are disappearing every year.

Surprisingly, the Internet may offer a solution to this problem. Although it is true that English dominates the Internet, the number of websites in other languages is growing very quickly. With chat sites and messenger programs people can communicate more easily than before and in any language they know. ⁵_____ .

a For example, approximately 70 percent of websites are in English.
b But almost one and a quarter billion people across the world use English as a second or foreign language.
c In the future students may have to learn global English.
d Not all languages are so successful, however.
e So perhaps modern technology can help save some languages from dying out.
f Some languages like Urdu or Hindi are growing much faster than English.

A English in the world ☐
B Languages around the world ☐
C The language of the Internet ☐

SPEAKING SKILLS

1 Roleplay the conversation.

Student A
While on holiday in the UK you see an advert for a camping trip to Brighton. You and your friend want to go. Call the tourist office and ask:
• if there are places available.
• how much the trip costs and how you are going to get there.
• things to do in Brighton and what you need to take with you.
You start the conversation.

Student B
You work in a tourist office in the UK. Someone calls you to ask about a camping trip to Brighton. Answer his/her questions and tell him/her about:
• the number of places available.
• the cost of the trip and the transport included.
• things to do in Brighton and what he/she needs to take with him/her.
Your partner starts the conversation.

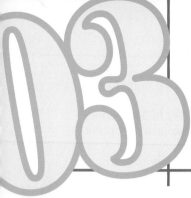

Growing up

Read, listen and talk about school; growing up.
Practise the Past Simple and *used to*; education vocabulary; adjectives with *-ed/-ing* endings.
Focus on asking for permission; predicting in reading and listening.
Write a personal recollection.

Kate Scott Year 11 — Creative writing

The best days of your life?

It was such a big day but I don't remember very much. It's like an impressionist painting: shapes, colours, and smells and sounds too. But I was only five years old and it was a long time ago!

I walked to school with Mum and I cried all the way. I didn't want to go. I had a blue rucksack and a big new box of crayons. The playground was full of noisy, excited kids. Some of the children looked huge – I never knew that I was so small! Then a bell rang and everybody stopped running and went inside. How did everybody know what to do?

The walls were yellow and there was a horrible smell of soap everywhere. My teacher's name was Mrs Bell. ('What a strange name!' I thought.) She wasn't very strict. In fact she was really nice but I didn't understand a lot of the things she said that day. Terms, timetables, registers, cloakrooms ... What did she mean? And why was her voice so loud all the time? It was very strange.

I don't remember what we learnt that day. I think we sang songs and clapped a lot. Mrs Bell read us a story and we sat cross-legged on the floor. I was embarrassed because I didn't know how to do it! There was also an aquarium with ugly fish in it – another horrible smell.

'So, Kate, were you a good girl today?' Dad asked me later.
'I don't know!' I said.
'Was it fun?'
'No! And Mrs Bell said that we have to go back tomorrow!' I wasn't very happy.
'Did you make any new friends?'
'Yes, I did. I think ...'
'Did you learn anything useful? Numbers? Colours?'
'Dad! Why are you asking me all these questions? Didn't you go to school?'

GRAMMAR AND READING

1 Look at the photo and answer the questions. Use the ideas below to help you.

- How old do you think the girl is?
- What is the situation? How do you know?
- How do you think she is feeling? Why?

primary school/playground/kids/
an important day
go with Mum/Dad
feel small/nervous/grown up/proud
wear new clothes/school uniform
make new friends/shout/laugh/run/cry

Work it out

2 **CD ROM** Read the text and answer the questions.

1 Is Kate talking about a present or past event?
2 What are the two forms of the verb *to be* in the Past Simple?
3 Find three regular Past Simple verbs. What are their infinitives?
4 Find three irregular Past Simple verbs. What are their infinitives?

3 Complete the sentences.

Present Simple	Past Simple
I **walk** to school.	I ¹_____ to school.
I **don't know** how to do it.	I ²_____ **know** how to do it.
Do you **learn** anything useful?	³_____ you **learn** anything useful?
Yes, I **do**./No, I **don't**.	Yes, I ⁴_____ ./No, I ⁵_____ .

Check it out

Past Simple		
We use the Past Simple to talk about things that started and finished in the past.		
	to be	Regular and irregular verbs
Affirmative	I **was** only five. The walls **were** yellow.	The children **looked** huge. We **sang** songs.
Negative	I **wasn't** very happy. They **weren't** very nice to me.	I **didn't want** to go. I **didn't know** how to do it.
Questions	**Was** it fun? Yes, it **was**./No it **wasn't**. **Were** you a good girl?	**Did** you **learn** anything useful? Yes, I **did**./No, I **didn't**. How **did** they **know** what to do?
Time expressions:	yesterday, last night/year/week/Saturday, when I was five, ten years ago, in 2004/1999, one day/morning	

4 Circle the irregular verb in each list and write its Past Simple form.

1 look / play / start / think _____
2 buy / decide / phone / work _____
3 rain / talk / forget / shout _____
4 listen / feel / visit / watch _____
5 stay / hate / promise / wear _____
6 live / give / invite / laugh _____

5 **CD 1.21** Listen and put the regular verbs in Exercise 4 in the correct column. Then practise saying them.

/d/	/t/	/ɪd/
played	looked	started

6 Write the questions in the Past Simple. Then look at Kate's story again and answer them.

1 How old/be/Kate?
2 Kate/walk to school/on her own?
3 What/everybody/do/when the bell rang?
4 What/be/Kate's teacher's name?
5 The teacher/strict?
6 Kate/enjoy/her first day at school?

7 Work in pairs. Use a time expression from Check it out and answer the questions.

When did you start primary /secondary school?
I started primary school when I was six/in 1995/11 years ago.

When did you last:
• see your grandparents?
I last saw my grandparents in March.
• check your email?
• cook a meal?
• laugh out loud at a film?
• go swimming?

8 **CD 1.22** Listen and match speakers 1–5 with questions a–e. Then listen again and check.

Speaker 1 ☐ Speaker 4 ☐
Speaker 2 ☐ Speaker 5 ☐
Speaker 3 ☐

a How did you spend the first day?
b Did you like your form tutor?
c Did you make any new friends?
d Were you scared before the first day?
e What did you wear?

9 Write a short description of your first day at secondary school. Follow the instructions.

• In pairs, answer questions a–e in Exercise 8. Make notes.
• Use your notes and the text in Exercise 2 to describe your day.

READING

1 Match the people below with pictures A–D. What were they famous for? Use the correct form of the verbs to complete the sentences about them.

propose   invent   paint   write

1 Thomas Alva Edison _____ the phonograph (the first record player). ☐
2 Leonardo da Vinci _____ the Mona Lisa. ☐
3 Agatha Christie _____ crime novels. ☐
4 Albert Einstein _____ the theory of relativity. ☐

Hidden talents

1 They often didn't learn to read and write until they were older. Their parents often thought they were stupid and their friends laughed at them. Some of them hated their schooldays and decided to drop out of school as soon as possible. In short, they had unhappy schooldays.

2 Some of the world's greatest composers, writers and inventors had an unpleasant time at school like this. Later, when they became successful, nobody was more surprised than their old classmates. Were these people stupid? No, of course not! Some people believe that they had something in common – dyslexia.

3 Dyslexia is a learning disability which means that people have problems with reading and remembering written words. It is often difficult for them to memorise things. Studies show that people with dyslexia use a different part of their brain to read and remember. Experts think that the cause of dyslexia is genetic: probably somebody else in the family also had dyslexia. Statistically, about 15 percent of people are dyslexic, but not everybody who has dyslexia knows about it.

4 Some people with dyslexia discover they have special, hidden talents, but only when they are older. A good example is Agatha Christie, one of the most successful writers in history – two billion books published in 44 languages! At school she had problems with writing and often got bad marks for essays. Her parents were disappointed and wanted Agatha to leave school early. She only started writing because her older sister said she couldn't do it! And even when she was already a famous crime writer, she sometimes felt embarrassed because she still couldn't spell.

5 There are many more examples of people like Agatha Christie: Hans Christian Andersen, Albert Einstein, Leonardo da Vinci, Pablo Picasso and Thomas Edison; important and creative people who had problems with reading and writing when they were young. Of course, that doesn't mean that everybody with dyslexia is a genius, but it shows that sometimes people can be a lot more intelligent than they seem.

2 Look at the pictures again and read the title of the text. What do you think it is about?

3 Read the first paragraph. What do you think the text is about now?

a unhappy children ☐
b people who had problems at school ☐
c the effects of bad education ☐
d people who became successful after they finished school ☐

4 Read the last paragraph only. Do you need to change your answer to Exercise 3?

5 Look at Exercises 2–4 and complete points a–d in Train Your Brain.

TRAIN YOUR BRAIN | Reading skills

Predicting

You can make a text easier to understand by predicting what it is going to be about before you read it. Always:

a look at the _____ .
b read the _____ .
c read the _____ paragraph of the text.
d read the _____ paragraph of the text.

6 (CD ROM) Now read the whole text. Did you predict the subject correctly?

7 Read the whole text again and match headings a–f with paragraphs 1–5. There's one heading you don't need.

a What is dyslexia? ☐
b Typical problems for children with dyslexia at school ☐
c How to help people with dyslexia ☐
d What some talented people had in common ☐
e Other famous people who had dyslexia ☐
f A person who had hidden talents ☐

8 Match definitions a–f with words and phrases in the text.

a (v) [para. 1] stop going to school/university _____
b (n) [para. 2] pupils in the same class at school _____
c (v) [para. 3] learn by heart _____
d (n) [para. 4] a score which shows how good a piece of work is _____
e (adj) [para. 4] unhappy because of poor results _____
f (adj) [para. 5] good at using your imagination _____

9 Read the text again and circle the correct answer.

1 The children in paragraph 1
a had a difficult time at school.
b had classmates who were stupid.
c left school early.

2 Some famous writers, composers and inventors
a were not very intelligent.
b were surprised when they became successful.
c had similar problems when they were children.

3 People with dyslexia
a were probably born with the disability.
b never knew about it.
c can't remember anything.

4 Agatha Christie started writing because
a her parents wanted her to.
b she wanted to show her sister that she could write.
c she wanted to leave school early.

5 The people mentioned in the last paragraph are
a not geniuses.
b crime writers like Agatha Christie.
c well-known people who had problems with reading and writing.

10 Work in pairs. Was there anything you were bad at when you were younger, but you can do now?

A I couldn't swim when I was younger, but now I am quite a good swimmer.
B I didn't understand Chemistry when I was younger but now I'm quite good at it.

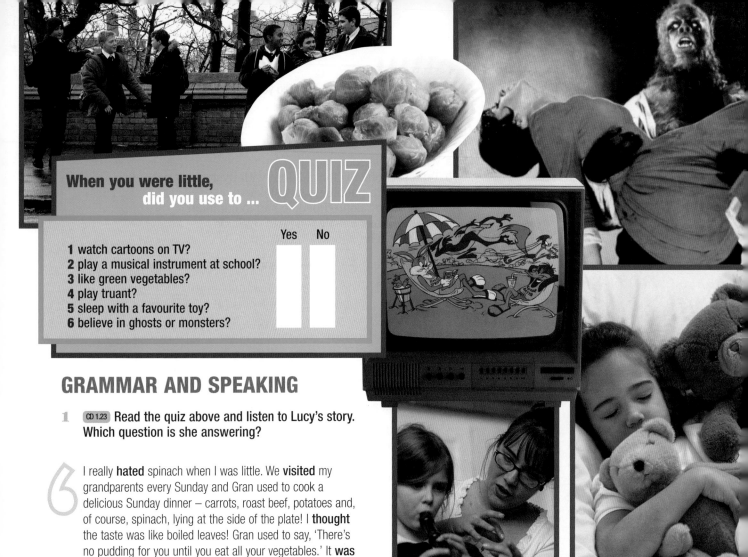

QUIZ

When you were little, did you use to ...

	Yes	No
1 watch cartoons on TV?		
2 play a musical instrument at school?		
3 like green vegetables?		
4 play truant?		
5 sleep with a favourite toy?		
6 believe in ghosts or monsters?		

GRAMMAR AND SPEAKING

1 **CD 1.23** Read the quiz above and listen to Lucy's story. Which question is she answering?

I really **hated** spinach when I was little. We **visited** my grandparents every Sunday and Gran used to cook a delicious Sunday dinner – carrots, roast beef, potatoes and, of course, spinach, lying at the side of the plate! I **thought** the taste was like boiled leaves! Gran used to say, 'There's no pudding for you until you eat all your vegetables.' It **was** horrible! One Sunday I **had** a clever idea to hide the spinach under my plate. But my sister **started** laughing and, of course, everybody **saw** me. It's funny, because I didn't use to like spinach but I love it now!

Work it out

2 **Look at the sentence and decide which explanation is correct.**

My gran used to cook a delicious Sunday dinner.

a Lucy's grandmother regularly cooked a Sunday dinner (but now she doesn't).
b Lucy's grandmother cooked a Sunday dinner only once.

Check it out

used to

Used to expresses a regular habit or state in the past which doesn't happen any more. We can't use *used to* if something happened only once.

My gran **used to** cook a delicious Sunday dinner.

I **didn't use to** like spinach.

Did you **use to** like green vegetables?
Yes, I **did**./No, I **didn't**.

3 **Correct the wrong sentences.**

1 We used to wear school uniforms.
2 She used to arrive late for class.
3 I used to fail my Maths exam last Friday.
4 I used to cycle to school every day.
5 Last summer, I used to break my leg.

4 **Read Lucy's story in Exercise 1. Which verbs in bold can we change to *used to* + infinitive?**

5 **Look at other changes in Lucy's life. Write sentences with *used to* and *didn't use to*.**

Lucy used to go to ballet lessons. She didn't use to go to bed late.

1 Lucy stopped
    going to ballet lessons.
    keeping a diary.
    listening to boy bands.

2 Lucy started
    going to bed late.
    listening to hip-hop.
    wearing lipstick.

6 **In pairs, ask and answer the questions in the quiz. Use *used to* or *didn't use to*.**

A Did you use to watch cartoons on TV?
B Yes, I did. My favourite cartoon was ... .

28

LISTENING

1 CD 1.24 Look at the picture below. Then listen to Part 1 of the recording and answer the questions.

- How old do you think the people are?
- Where are they?
- How well do you know each other?

2 CD 1.25 Listen to Part 2 of the recording and answer the questions.

1 What sort of party is it?
 a a birthday party
 b a reunion party
 c a house-warming party
2 Which words help you to decide on the answer to question 1?

3 CD 1.25 Listen again and tick the expressions you hear.

1 **Remember me?**
2 Good to see you.
3 **How are you?**
4 I can't believe it!
5 **Pleased to meet you.**
6 What a surprise!
7 **I didn't recognise you.**
8 So, what's new?

4 Work in pairs. What do you think the characters are going to talk about? Make a list of topics. Then compare it with another pair.

5 CD 1.26 Listen to Part 3 of the recording and check your ideas from Exercise 4.

6 In pairs, put the advice in Train Your Brain in the correct order. Look at Exercises 1–4 to help you.

TRAIN YOUR BRAIN | Listening skills

Predicting

a Listen for key words which give you clues about the situation. ☐
b Look at the pictures or photos. ☐
c Think about the situation and try to guess what the people are going to talk about. ☐

---

7 CD 1.27 Listen to Part 4 of the recording. What job is Ben doing now? Listen again. Tick true and cross false.

1 Jake isn't interested in astronomy any more. ☐
2 Jake is a father now. ☐
3 At school, Ben's plan was to be a lawyer. ☐
4 Ben didn't finish his university course. ☐
5 Ben likes his job because the routine is the same every day. ☐
6 Ben doesn't like the people he works with. ☐
7 When Ben was little, he wanted to be a postman. ☐

8 Work in groups. Ask each other these questions.

1 When you were a child, what job did you want to have?
2 What do you want to study in the future?
A When I was a child I wanted to be a rock star.
B Really? I wanted to be a doctor.

9 Work in groups. Imagine you are at a school reunion party in ten years' time. Use the expressions in Exercise 3. Ask other people in the group:

- what job they have now.
- about their families.
- about people they remember from school.

A So, Mark, what job do you have now?
B I'm a pilot …

VOCABULARY

1 **Think Back!** In pairs, add as many adjectives as you can to the lists.

Adjectives with *-ing* endings	Adjectives with *-ed* endings
embarrassing	embarrassed
frightening	frightened
disappointing	disappointed
annoying	annoyed

Mind the trap!

If a thing, person or situation is ...	boring, interesting, annoying,	you feel ...	bored. interested. annoyed.

2 Circle the correct answer.

1 I felt very *exciting / excited* before my first day at secondary school.
2 Mrs Jones was a very strict teacher – we were *terrifying / terrified* of her.
3 Studying before exams is always very *tiring / tired*.
4 She felt *surprising / surprised* when she passed all her exams.
5 This textbook is very *boring / bored*.
6 I was *amazing / amazed* that all the other children knew what to do.
7 Are you *interesting / interested* in computers?

3 Complete the sentences. Make adjectives from the verbs in capital letters.

1 This school has hundreds of _____ pupils.   SATISFY
2 The idea of becoming a pilot was very _____ .   EXCITE
3 I was never _____ when I visited my grandparents.   BORE
4 The view from the top floor was _____.   AMAZE
5 I thought that tractors were _____ when I was young!   FASCINATE
6 That film was absolutely _____.   TERRIFY
7 I failed my Maths test. I felt very _____.   EMBARRASS
8 I forgot to bring my umbrella. It was very _____.   ANNOY

4 Look at the questions and tell your partner how you felt.

I felt terrified before my last English test.

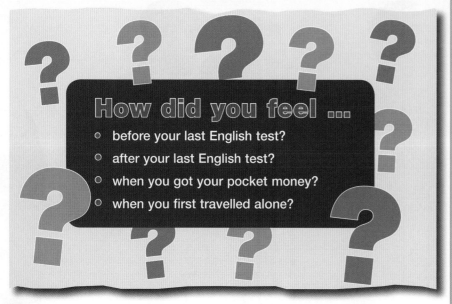

How did you feel ...

- before your last English test?
- after your last English test?
- when you got your pocket money?
- when you first travelled alone?

SPEAKING

1 In pairs, look at the photo. Try and guess the answers to the questions.

1 Where are they?
2 What do you think the problem is?

2 **CD 1.28** Listen to the conversation. Were your answers to Exercise 1 correct?

3 **CD 1.28** Listen again. Which things does the student ask to borrow? Make a list.

4 **CD 1.29** Study Speak Out. Then follow the instructions.

- Listen and tick the phrases you hear.
- In which of the three conversations does the speaker sound rude? Why?
- Listen to the other two conversations again and practise saying them with a partner.

6 In pairs, look at the signs and questions. Then think of possible answers.

Can I take the lift?

Can I ride my bike here?

Is it OK if I go in here?

Is it OK if I wear my trainers here?

Do you mind if I use my mobile phone?

SPEAK OUT | Asking for, giving and refusing permission

Question	*Yes*	*No* + reason (Always give a reason when you say *no*.)
Can I borrow your dictionary? **Is it OK if I** smoke?	Yes, of course. Sure, no problem.	Sorry, you can't. I'm using it. I'm afraid not. It's not allowed.
Do you mind if I open the window? **Do you mind if I** turn the TV off?	No, please do. No, I don't mind.	I'm afraid I do. It's a bit cold. Yes, I do. I'm watching it.

Mind the trap!

Do you mind if ...? = Is it a problem for you if ...?

If somebody asks you a question starting with *Do you mind if ...?* and it isn't a problem, you should answer *No* (= No, it isn't a problem.)
Do you mind if I sit here? **No**, I don't./**No**, please do.

5 In pairs, ask for and give or refuse permission. Choose from the ideas below.

borrow your watch/your shoes/a piece of paper/…
use your glasses/dictionary/…
visit you tonight/keep your pen …
ask you a question/for your phone number/…

A Is it OK if I take your chair?
B No, I'm sorry, you can't. I need it!

7 In pairs, make a dialogue for each situation.

1 You're at your friend's house. You suddenly remember that you promised to phone your mother. You don't have a mobile phone.
2 The train is very full. A family is sitting together and there is one free space in the middle of them.
3 You need to leave class early today.

Inspiration

Read, listen and talk about artists and writers; inspiration; important moments.
Practise the Past Simple and the Past Continuous; time expressions.
Focus on recounting past events; phrasal verbs.
Write about past events.

GRAMMAR AND LISTENING

1 CD 1.30 Listen to these three pieces of music. Which one do you like best? Which adjectives could describe each piece?

- *Rhapsody in Blue* by George Gershwin
- *Moonlight Sonata* by Ludwig van Beethoven
- *The Cat Waltz* by Frederic Chopin

exciting boring dramatic mysterious
melodic catchy irritating sentimental

2 Read anecdotes A–C below and match them to the pictures 1–3.

Work it out

3 Match sentences 1 and 2 with uses of the Past Continuous a and b.

1 Night was falling and the Moon was shining.
2 Late one evening Chopin was composing in his music room.

a setting the scene at the beginning of a story
b saying that somebody was in the middle of an action at a particular time

4 Look at the sentence and answer the questions.

While Gershwin was travelling by train, he suddenly got the idea for *Rhapsody in Blue*.

1 Did these actions happen
   a one after another?
   b at the same time?
2 Which action was shorter and which tense do we use to talk about it?

Eureka moments!

1

2

A One day in the 1920s, the great American composer George Gershwin was travelling to a concert in Boston. While he was sitting alone on the train, he suddenly got the idea for his most famous work, *Rhapsody in Blue*. When you listen to the music today, you can clearly hear the train wheels and the whistle!

B Night was falling and the Moon was shining. Beethoven was walking around Vienna – he was looking for inspiration. As he was passing a small house, he heard one of his compositions. Somebody was playing it on the piano but kept on making mistakes. Beethoven was intrigued and decided to find out who it was. He entered the house and realised that the girl at the piano was blind. He sat and played music to her for over an hour. Suddenly the Moon appeared at the window. Beethoven was excited by the special atmosphere in the room and began to compose his famous *Moonlight Sonata*.

Check it out

Past Continuous

We use the Past Continuous:

- to set the scene, often at the start of a story.
  Night was falling and the Moon was shining.

- to talk about what was happening at a particular moment in the past.
  At ten o'clock he was composing in his music room.

- with the Past Simple to show that a long activity was interrupted by a short one. We usually use *while* or *as* before the Past Continuous.
  While/As he was sitting at the piano, a small kitten suddenly ran across the piano keys.

Affirmative	I/He/She was listening. We/You/They were listening.
Negative	I/He/She wasn't listening. We/You/They weren't listening.
Questions	Was I/he/she listening? Yes, I/he/she was./No, I/he/she wasn't. Were you/we/they listening? Yes, you/ we/they were./No, you/we/they weren't.

3

C In the summer of 1837, the Polish composer Chopin was living in Paris. Late one evening he was composing alone in his music room. While he was sitting at the piano, a small kitten suddenly ran across the piano keys. Chopin liked the strange melody and he tried to write it down. In 1838, he published a new composition. The title? – *The Cat Waltz*!

5 Look at the pictures and the texts again. Correct the sentences.

1 Gershwin was smoking a cigar.
2 Gershwin was travelling with friends to Boston.
3 In 1837, Chopin was living in Warsaw.
4 Late in the evening, Chopin was reading in his music room.
5 Beethoven was walking around Vienna in the morning.
6 Somebody was playing one of Beethoven's compositions on the violin.

6 Complete the sentences with the correct form of the Past Simple or the Past Continuous.

The composer Rossini [1] _____ (write) many operatic masterpieces like *The Barber of Seville*. He was famous for composing his music at the last minute. Sometimes, just an hour before a concert Rossini [2] _____ (still write) the music for it! Rossini was also famous for composing in unusual situations – for example, he [3] _____ (get) the idea for the beginning of his opera *Le Comte Ory* while he [4] _____ (fish) with a friend.

7 Complete the sentences. Use the Past Simple or the Past Continuous.

1 I _____ (read) my brother's diary when he suddenly _____ (come) into the room!
2 Where _____ (you/go) when I _____ (see) you last night?
3 When I _____ (wake) up this morning, it _____ (snow).
4 I _____ (drop) my mobile while I _____ (text) my friend.
5 _____ (you/sleep) when I _____ (phone) this morning?
6 He _____ (not look) where he _____ (go) and _____ (crash) into a tree.

8 What do you think your partner was doing at these times? Ask and check if your guesses were correct.

ten o'clock last night   six o'clock this morning
last Saturday at 8p.m.

A Were you sleeping at ten o'clock last night?
B No, I wasn't. I was studying Chemistry!

9 **CD 1.31** Listen and write sentences. Use the prompts and the Past Simple and the Past Continuous.

watch the football match   start to rain
robbers break into the house   sleep
have a bath   have a picnic   play the guitar
have a good idea   complain   ring

1 While he was watching the football match, his phone rang.

Why sleep is the best medicine

by David Flak

It's late at night and you have an important exam in the morning. You're sitting with your notes and books and you're beginning to feel tired. Should you listen to your mother's advice and go to bed? Or should you stay up all night and try to learn?

Well, scientists say that our mothers are probably right – it's best to go to bed early before a big exam. Last year in Germany, scientists looked into the effects of sleep on university students. They found out that students who had at least four hours of sleep did better in exams. It also turned out that the students who had a lot of sleep had better scores in IQ tests. So why is sleep good for our brains?

First of all, scientists believe that after a hard day of thinking, our memories are very messy. Sleep helps to tidy up our thoughts and memories and to put everything in the right place again. Because of this, it's easier to remember facts clearly, which, of course, is important in exams.

When we sleep, our brains also continue thinking about our problems from the day before. We can sometimes come up with the answers to difficult problems after sleeping. There are many examples of this in history.

In the nineteenth century, the chemical structure of benzene was still a big mystery to scientists. The German chemist Friedrich von Kekulé worked on this problem for many years. One afternoon, while he was travelling on a London bus, von Kekulé fell asleep. He had a strange dream – snakes were coming towards him with their tails in their mouths! When he woke up, von Kekulé knew that he had the answer to his problem – the atoms were arranged in a circle like his funny snakes!

But sleep does not only improve our memories and help us to find the answer to problems. Scientists believe that we are more creative after sleep too. Keith Richards, the guitarist of The Rolling Stones, came up with the melody for *Satisfaction*, their biggest hit, as he was taking a nap in a London hotel room. The Irish writer Bram Stoker also got the idea for his masterpiece *Dracula*, the classic horror story, while he was sleeping. He ate crabs late at night before going to bed, had some strange nightmares and kept on waking up!

So, take my advice – do you want to remember more in your exam tomorrow? The answer is simple – go to bed early!

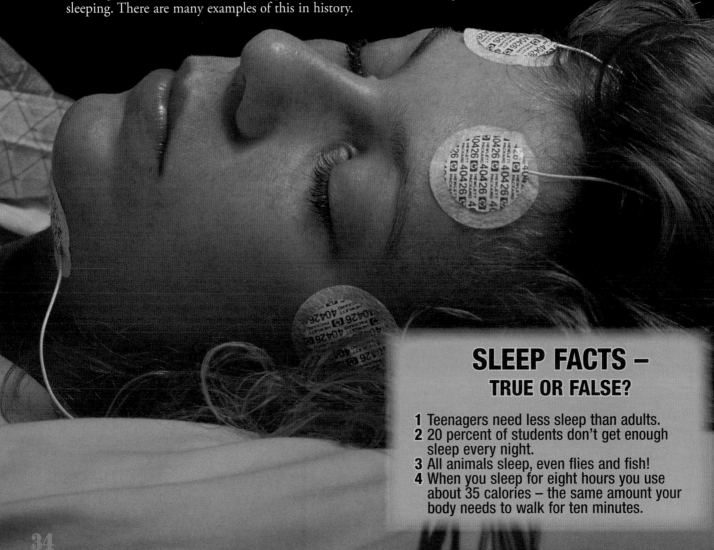

SLEEP FACTS –
TRUE OR FALSE?

1 Teenagers need less sleep than adults.
2 20 percent of students don't get enough sleep every night.
3 All animals sleep, even flies and fish!
4 When you sleep for eight hours you use about 35 calories – the same amount your body needs to walk for ten minutes.

READING AND VOCABULARY

1 Read the Sleep Facts. In pairs, decide which facts are true. Check your answers on page 140.

2 Read the first and the last paragraph of the article, look at the title and the photo and decide what the article is about.

    a How sleep helps us when we're ill.
    b The effects of sleep on our brains.
    c How sleep can make us more beautiful.

3 **CD ROM** Read the article. Was your answer to Exercise 2 correct?

4 Find sentences in the text which tell you the information below.

    1 Scientists agree with what our parents tell us about sleep.
    2 Experiments show that sleep can help you do well in tests.
    3 Sleep organises memories and facts in our brains.
    4 At night our brains don't stop thinking about things from the previous day.
    5 Sleep can help us to solve difficult problems.
    6 Sleep can be good for the imagination.

5 In pairs, answer the questions without looking at the text.

    1 Where was the German chemist sleeping when he solved a scientific mystery?
    2 What did the guitarist of The Rolling Stones compose while he was sleeping in a hotel?
    3 What kind of story did the Irish writer invent while he was sleeping?

6 Look at the photo on page 140. In pairs, answer the questions. Use the ideas below to help you.

    stay up late   tired   sleepy   stressed
    drink coffee   revising before an exam
    learn facts by heart

    1 What is the person doing? Why?
    2 How do you think he is feeling?
    3 When do you study best? Early in the morning or late in the evening?
    4 Before an important exam, do you prefer to study all night or have a good night's sleep?
    5 How many hours do you normally sleep every night? Is it enough?

VOCABULARY

1 **Think Back!** Look at the article. Write the missing verbs in these sentences.

    come   tidy   turn   keep   stay   look   find

    1 At the end of the film, it _____ out that the couple used to be married to each other.
    2 I'm really tired this morning – I _____ on making mistakes.
    3 I'm trying to _____ up with an idea for my essay.
    4 Sleep helps to _____ up our memories.
    5 To _____ out more about sleep, visit our website.
    6 It's not a good idea to _____ up all night and study.
    7 Last year scientists decided to _____ into the effects of sleep on university students.

2 Write the correct phrasal verb from Exercise 1 next to its definition.

    a happen (often in an unexpected way) _turn out_
    b put something where it should be _____
    c get some information _____
    d think of (an idea) _____
    e investigate _____
    f continue doing something; do something many times _____
    g not go to bed _____

3 Complete the sentences with a phrasal verb in the correct tense.

    1 She _____ the idea for the book while she was travelling by train.
    2 I can't find anything! I need to _____ my bedroom!
    3 Martin's sleepy today – he _____ and chatted all night on the Internet.
    4 I was worried because my essay was terrible – but it _____ that it was fine!
    5 At the moment, scientists _____ how caffeine wakes us up.
    6 We need to _____ how much the tickets cost – let's phone them tomorrow.
    7 My boss is really angry with me – I _____ coming to work late.

4 Choose three phrasal verbs from Exercise 1. Write your own sentence for each verb.

SPEAKING AND LISTENING

1 **CD 1.32** Listen to Monica, Jonathan and Lee. Match speakers 1–3 with events a–c.

1 Jonathan ☐ a The attack on the World Trade Center
2 Lee ☐ b The first man on the Moon
3 Monica ☐ c The day of the exam results

2 **Read Jonathan's story and answer the questions.**

1 Which phrases does Jonathan use to say when the story happened?
2 Which time expressions does he use to talk about each step in the story?
3 Which sentences contain both the Past Simple and the Past Continuous?
4 Which adjectives does he use to describe how he was feeling?
5 Which words does he use to end his story?

It was in 1969. I was about five years old. My brother and I were sleeping and Mum came to wake us up. We didn't really know what was happening. We got dressed and after that we went downstairs. It was the middle of the night – we felt really grown-up! We ran into the living room and we saw that the whole family was waiting for us – my mum, my dad and my grandparents. Then my Dad switched on our new colour TV. I still remember his face. He looked so proud! After that we sat and watched – the pictures weren't very clear but I remember Neil Armstrong was doing a funny sort of dance. And the Earth looked very small and blue. Nobody spoke – we were so excited. I think the whole world was watching that evening. Finally the programme ended and we went back to bed. But I couldn't sleep. It was an unforgettable night.

3 **CD 1.33** Choose an adjective to describe the speaker's feelings in each situation. Then listen and check your answers.

surprised   pleased   excited   shocked
worried   proud   stupid   irritated

1 I started dancing around the room. _____
2 Suddenly the plane started shaking and going up and down. _____
3 It turned out I had the best results in the class. _____
4 I was waiting for four hours at the Passport Office. _____

4 **Put these time expressions in the correct place in the table.**

It was in 2001.   Eventually   After that
It happened three years ago.   Finally
Then   Later   Next

Beginning of the story	The next stages of the story	The end of the story
It was in 2001.	Next	Eventually
_____	_____	
	_____	
	_____	

5 **CD 1.34** Put Lee's story in the correct order. Then listen and check.

a It happened six years ago. I remember the date very well. It was 11 September 2001. I was in my first year of secondary school. ☐
b Finally I found some information about the attack on the World Trade Center. I was so shocked. It was an unforgettable day. ☐
c After that I ran home, turned on my computer and then I started surfing the Internet. ☐
d While I was walking the dog, my mobile rang. It was my friend Matt. 'Lee! Did you hear the news? I can't believe it!' he said. I didn't know what he was talking about! ☐

SPEAK OUT | Recounting a past event

Say when the story happened.
**It happened a few years ago./It was in [+ year].
I was about … years old./I was in my first year of secondary school./I was visiting … .**

Use the linking words to talk about each stage of the story.
Then/After that/Next/Finally

Use the Past Continuous when two actions happened at the same time.
As/While **I was leaving** the house, I suddenly remembered that … .

Say how you felt.
I felt surprised/pleased/excited … .

Say why this day/event is important.
**It was an unforgettable day … .
To this day I'm proud of/afraid of … .
It was the best/worst day of my life.**

6 **Study Speak Out. Then, in pairs, choose from these ideas and talk about day.**

A day when you:
• heard some news that was important for your country/the world.
• were very lucky or unlucky.
• got some good/bad news (exam results, a relationship, death of somebody famous …).
• suddenly had a good idea.

LISTENING

1 Work in pairs and answer the questions.

- Who is your favourite poet?
- How much do you know about him/her?
- Who are the most famous poets in your country's literature? Do you like their poetry? Why?/Why not?

2 Read the extract from Coleridge's biography. Why do you think he didn't finish his famous poem?

Samuel Taylor Coleridge

Samuel Taylor Coleridge was one of England's great poets. He was born in 1772, studied at Cambridge University but he gave up before the end of his studies. Together with his friend Wordsworth, Coleridge became one of the most important romantic poets in England. One of Coleridge's most famous poems was *Kubla Khan* – a fantastic vision of an exotic palace. While he was writing the poem, somebody

3 CD 1.35 Listen to the story. Was your prediction in Exercise 2 correct?

4 CD 1.35 In pairs, put the story in the correct order. Compare your answers with another pair. Then listen again and check.

a As he was listening to the stranger at the door, Coleridge began to forget his dream. ☐

b Coleridge decided to spend the night in a lonely farmhouse. ☐1

c He didn't finish his poem. ☐

d He had an amazing dream while he was sleeping. ☐

e He wasn't feeling well and took some medicine at bedtime. ☐

f He read a book and fell asleep. ☐

g A stranger knocked at the door. ☐

h He began to write a poem about his dream. ☐

5 CD 1.35 How much can you remember? In pairs, circle the correct answer. Listen again and check.

1 The story happened in the *eighteenth / nineteenth* century.

2 Coleridge was travelling *with friends / on his own*.

3 Coleridge took some medicine and read a book *in bed / by the fire*.

4 Coleridge had a fantastic dream about *a palace / a farmhouse*.

5 Coleridge *invited the stranger into the house / talked to the stranger at the front door*.

6 After he listened to the man for an hour, Coleridge felt very *irritated / worried*.

7 When the man from Porlock left, Coleridge remembered *nothing / very little* from his dream.

6 In pairs, tell the story about Coleridge. Use your answers to Exercises 4 and 5 and Speak Out on page 36 to help you.

What did they do?

Philo Farnsworth

A

A boy was working on his parents' farm in America. He was fourteen. While he was working in a field, he had an idea for sending pictures through the air. He told his teacher about it and asked some businessmen for money. He took the money and opened a laboratory. In 1927 he showed the first working television system.

B

1 The story begins in 1921. Philo Farnsworth, a poor 14-year-old American boy, was helping his mother and father on the family farm in Idaho.

2 While he was working in one of the fields of potatoes, he suddenly had a fantastic idea. As he was looking at the lines of potatoes in the field, he realised that you could send pictures in similar lines through the air and then put them together again at the other end.

3 Farnsworth was very excited and he ran to see his old high school Science teacher after work. He told his teacher about his idea and after that started drawing pictures of his idea on the blackboard. His teacher was amazed! Next he talked to some local businessmen and asked them to give him some money. Later he used the money to open a small laboratory in California.

4 Finally, in 1927, Farnsworth was the first person to show a working television system.

WRITING

1 Look at the photos on page 38. What do you think Philo Farnsworth invented?

2 Read story A. Was your answer to Exercise 1 correct?

3 In pairs, read another version B of the story. Which version is better? Why? Give four reasons. Then compare your answers with another pair.

4 In pairs, read story B again. Answer the questions. Then check your answers in Train Your Brain.

   1 What was happening at the beginning of the story? What tense describes this?
   2 Which paragraph(s):
      a sets the scene? ☐
      b develop the narrative? ☐ ☐
      c tells us what the conclusion is? ☐
   3 Which words are used to introduce the next parts of the story? Underline them.
   4 Can you find any adjectives in the story? Why are they important?

TRAIN YOUR BRAIN | Writing skills

Past events

a Use the Past Continuous to describe what was happening at the beginning of the story.
b Remember to use paragraphs for each new part of the story.
c Use linking words (*then*, *after that*, *finally*) for the next parts of the story.
d Use some adjectives to make your writing more interesting.

5 Look at the pictures on the right. Match verbs and expressions (a–e) with the pictures (1–5).

   a think about the falling apple for many years ☐
   b publish his *Theory of Gravitation*/one of the most important books in the history of science ☐
   c one afternoon in 1665/rest under an apple tree ☐
   d suddenly/come up with the answer/excited/ start writing a book about it ☐
   e sleep/an apple/fall on his head ☐

6 Use Train Your Brain and the verbs and expressions above to write Newton's story.

VOCABULARY AND GRAMMAR

1 Circle the correct word.

1 The kids at school were running in the *aquarium / playground / uniform*.
2 I used to be *annoyed / terrified / terrifying* of my Maths teacher.
3 I lost the keys but *finally / first / next* I found them in my pocket.
4 I passed my Physics exam. I felt really *pleased / stupid / fascinated*.
5 I was so tired that I fell *asleep / blind / stressed* during the exam.
6 Scientists are still trying to *improve / solve / invent* this problem.

2 Complete the text with the correct form of the phrasal verbs in the box.

come up   find out   keep on   stay up
turn out   write down

I usually go to bed early, but yesterday I
¹_____ very late. I had to write a story
for my school magazine, and I was trying to
²_____ with a good idea. It wasn't
easy. I ³_____ lots of ideas, but they
weren't very good. I ⁴_____ thinking
of stories from films or books. Nothing original.
Suddenly, I heard a strange noise. I wanted to
⁵_____ what it was, so I turned the
light off and looked outside. It ⁶_____
that it was only a cat. But now I had an idea for
my story. I started writing.

3 Complete the sentences with the correct form of the words in capital letters.

1 Beethoven was a great _____ .   COMPOSE
2 Take my _____ and go to
  bed early.   ADVISE
3 The film was really _____ .   BORE
4 This is a very _____ story.   DRAMA
5 To be a writer, you need to have
  a good _____ .   IMAGINE
6 I went to Paris last year – it was
  an _____ holiday!   FORGET

4 Rewrite the sentences using the words in brackets so that they have the same meaning as the original sentences.

1 I don't go to a public school any more.
_____ (USED)
2 Did the teachers punish the children a lot?
_____ ? (STRICT)
3 I'm a good student now, but I wasn't before.
_____ (USE)
4 I went into the room. The man was shouting.
_____ (WHEN)
5 I was writing the last answer. The teacher told me to stop.
_____ (WHILE)
6 I passed all of my exams.
_____ (FAIL)

5 Complete the text with the correct form of the verbs in brackets.

Hi Helen!
How's it going? It's a pity you ¹_____ (cannot)
come to the party last night. There ²_____ (be)
about twenty people there and we had a great time.
In fact, at 3 o'clock we ³_____ (still dance)!
Everybody was wondering where you were. It didn't
seem fair that you ⁴_____ (study) when we were
enjoying ourselves! By the way, ⁵_____ (you/finish)
your project last night?
Anyway, I'm sure you're dying to hear the gossip.
When I got to the party, Paul ⁶_____ (dance)
with Abby! I was so surprised. Why ⁷_____
(he/dance) with her? Where was Mandy? Just then
Mandy ⁸_____ (walk) through the door with
Kenny. They ⁹_____ (hold) hands and looked as
if they were in love. I was disappointed because I
really like Kenny, but then I ¹⁰_____ (meet) this
really cool guy. It turned out he was Kenny's
brother! He's great. I'll tell you all about it tonight.
Take care – and don't work too hard!
Best wishes,
Emma

PRONUNCIATION

1 CD 1.36 Read the words. In each group circle the word that has a different vowel sound. Then listen and check.

1 all / car / floor / more
2 first / shirt / start / work
3 bath / form / mark / guard
4 bored / door / turn / store
5 four / heard / sir / term
6 word / bar / heart / laugh

LISTENING SKILLS

1 CD 1.37 Listen to the radio programme. Complete sentences 1–3 with the names in the box. Then match dreams 1–3 with interpretations a–c.

Helen   Tim   Jane

1 In _____'s dream he/she was flying.   ☐
2 In _____'s dream he/she couldn't get
  out of a room.   ☐
3 In _____'s dream he/she was doing a
  very difficult exam.   ☐

a You were feeling trapped. You were in a new
  situation but you weren't happy.
b You had a challenge in your life but you
  weren't very optimistic about it. You were
  worried because you thought you weren't
  doing enough.
c You were feeling happy because your life was
  changing and you felt free.

Penicillin – The Miracle Drug

In 1928, Alexander Fleming, a Scottish doctor and scientist, was working at a hospital in London. He was trying to find ways to fight bacteria. At that time many people died because of bacterial infections; sometimes from very small cuts.

Fleming was studying a dangerous bacteria called staphylococci. He was in a hurry because he was going to go on holiday, so he forgot to wash all his equipment in the laboratory before he left. There was one dish in which staphylococci was growing.

When Fleming came back from holiday a few weeks later, he noticed that there was something in the dish. He didn't know what the thing was, but he saw that it was stopping the harmful staphylococci bacteria from growing. Fleming called it penicillin.

He knew that penicillin could be an important discovery, and so he did some experiments with it. However, Fleming was not a chemist and he found it difficult to make pure penicillin. He asked some scientific colleagues to help him, but nobody seemed interested in producing penicillin. Fleming had to wait more than ten years before two brilliant scientists, Howard Florey and Ernst Chain finally found an easy way to produce the drug.

By May 1940, Florey's research team had enough penicillin to experiment with animals for the first time. In a simple experiment they gave a dangerous bacteria to eight mice. One hour later, they gave penicillin to only four of the mice. After a few hours the four mice with penicillin were fine, but the other four were all dead! When Florey heard of the result the next day he said, 'It looks like a miracle!'

During World War II penicillin saved many lives, and in 1945 Fleming, Florey and Chain won the Nobel Prize for medicine.

READING SKILLS

1 **Read the text and choose the correct answers.**

1 In 1928, Alexander Fleming
   a was studying bacteria.
   b had a bacterial infection.
   c cut people to stop them from dying.

2 Alexander Fleming discovered penicillin
   a while he was on holiday.
   b because he forgot to wash a dish.
   c when he was a student.

3 Fleming couldn't produce penicillin easily because
   a he didn't think it was important.
   b his colleagues didn't want him to.
   c he didn't know how to do it.

4 The first experiment with penicillin on animals was
   a extremely successful.
   b dangerous.
   c disappointing.

5 What is the text about?
   a How we use penicillin today.
   b The story of the discovery of penicillin.
   c The day Alexander Fleming discovered penicillin.

SPEAKING SKILLS

1 **In pairs, decide what to say in these situations.**

1 You are in an exam and you haven't got a pen. You call the teacher over.
2 You are on a hot city bus. All the windows are closed. There is an old man sitting next to you.
3 You are eating in a restaurant. The person at the next table asks you if she can smoke.
4 A friend asks you if you can lend him your MP3 player.
5 An old woman in the street asks you if she can use your mobile phone.

2 **Roleplay the conversation.**

Student A
You are talking with a friend about your memories from primary school. Tell him/her about your best day at school. Say:
• what happened and when it happened.
• how you felt.
• why that day was important for you.
You start the conversation. Then listen to your friend's story.

Student B
You are talking with a friend about your memories from primary school. Listen to your friend's story and then tell him/her about your worst day at school. Say:
• what happened and when it happened.
• how you felt.
• why that day was important for you.
Your partner starts the conversation.

No place like home

Read, listen and talk about houses and homes.
Practise comparative and superlative adjectives; relative pronouns.
Focus on describing photos; vocabulary connected with houses and homes.
Write a description.

GRAMMAR AND READING

1 In pairs, look at the picture of the houses and answer the questions.

- How many families do you think live here?
- Is this kind of house common in your country?

2 Tick the things you can see in the picture of the houses.

garden wall ☐   hedge ☐   garage ☐
statue ☐   front door ☐   skylight ☐
fountain ☐   drive ☐

3 CD ROM Read Chris's story. Which house did he live in, number 22 or number 24?

TRUE LIFE STORY | **Neighbours from hell!**

Semi-detached
Chris Austin talks about his neighbour nightmare

Our family used to have quite a good relationship with the Coopers next door. But the real problems with our neighbours started when they changed their front door. Mr Cooper said it was the most elegant front door in the street. Well, Mum was really angry that our door wasn't as elegant as theirs, so we bought a new one too. Then Dad painted the house and he boasted that the Coopers' wasn't as attractive as ours. So Mr Cooper painted his house too and at the same time he fitted more expensive windows. After that things just got worse and worse! Mum was always complaining that our house wasn't big enough, so Dad finally built an extra bedroom in the attic – and so did the Coopers. The Coopers also bought a better car (the largest Range Rover on the market!) and built a garage for it. Dad wasn't pleased that our car was older than theirs. The craziest thing happened two years ago. The Coopers bought a statue for the garden. Dad wasn't pleased that the Coopers' garden was prettier than ours, so he bought an enormous fountain. This was too much for the Coopers – they finally moved to a larger house. It's a pity because their daughter was really nice.

Chris Austin, Nottingham

Work it out

4 Match the sentences that have the same meaning.

1 The house was not as attractive as theirs.
2 The house was too small.
3 The house was not big enough.
4 The house was uglier than theirs.

5 Find comparative and superlative adjectives in the text opposite and add them to the box.

Comparison of adjectives			
	Adjective	Comparative	Superlative
One syllable	old large	1 _____ larg**er**	the old**est** 6 _____
Two syllables ending in -y	crazy pretty	craz**ier** 2 _____	7 _____ the pretti**est**
Two or more syllables	expensive elegant	3 _____ more elegant	the most expensive 8 _____
Irregular	good bad far	4 _____ 5 _____ further	the best the worst the furthest
Other ways of comparing:	too cold = not hot enough not as expensive (as) = cheaper (than)		

6 Read and complete the letter with the correct forms of the adjectives in brackets. Can you guess who Jacky is?

Dear Chris,

I'm writing to you from our new address. We're still unpacking - there's so much to do. Mum and Dad are very pleased because they think the new house is ¹ _____ (large) and ² _____ (comfortable) than our old one. Mum is already saying that it's ³ _____ (attractive) house in the neighbourhood. But as you know, my parents can be terrible snobs sometimes!

I'm not so sure that the move was a good decision. The garden's much ⁴ _____ (small) than our old one. We're a little ⁵ _____ (near) the city centre but it's ⁶ _____ (far) from school, so I get home ⁷ _____ (late) in the evenings and I have to get up ⁸ _____ (early) in the mornings too!

I hope we can still see each other I know my parents didn't get on very well with yours but I really like you. You're one of the ⁹ _____ (friendly) people I know.

Please write.

Love, Jacky x

S.W.A.L.K

7 Read the letter again. Tick the true sentences and correct the false ones.

1 The new house is not as large as the old one.
The new house is larger than the old one.
2 The new house isn't as comfortable as the old one.
3 The garden isn't as large as the old one.
4 The new house isn't as close to the city centre as the old one.
5 The house isn't as far from Jacky's school as the old one.
6 Jacky doesn't get back from school as late as she used to.

8 Write new sentences with the same meaning. Use the prompts and the adjectives below.

wide   low   long   quiet   warm   expensive

1 The room is too cold.
It's <u>not warm</u> enough.
2 The ceiling isn't high enough.
It's too _____.
3 The bed is too short.
It's _____ enough.
4 The radio isn't loud enough.
It's too _____.
5 The garage door is too narrow.
It's _____ enough.
6 The house isn't cheap enough.
It's too _____.

9 Work in groups and answer the questions.

In your group who lives:
• closest to school?
• furthest from school?
• in the noisiest/quietest part of the town/village?
• in the newest flat/house?

GRAMMAR AND LISTENING

1 Read the email and answer the questions.

- Where does Sanne come from?
- Where is she at the moment?
- What is she doing there?

2 Match the titles of the attachments 1–4 from Sanne's email with the photos A–D.

1 Robbie ☐
2 How does this work? ☐
3 The Colliers' Villa ☐
4 Custard ☐

Send | Save Draft | Attach ▾ | ⬆ ⬇ | Tools ▾ | ✕ Cancel

To: monica@fr.net

Subject: Hi from Hampstead

Hi Monica!

How are you? Just a quick note to say that I'm fine. I arrived in London late on Thursday. The Colliers met me at the airport. They're the couple **whose** son I'm looking after. Mr Collier's a lawyer and he's really nice. Mrs Collier is a teacher and she's very strict! But Charles is really sweet – he has got a lot of little friends **who** come to play with him in the afternoons. I love being a childminder.

The Colliers live in a villa in a quiet street in Hampstead. Hampstead is a district in North London **where** a lot of rich people live! In fact, nearly everyone **that** lives here is an actor or a rock star! I even saw Hugh Grant yesterday (I think)!

England's very different from the Netherlands though. I still don't know how to use the taps in the bathroom. And I don't like the food very much, although one thing **that** I really love here is custard – it's a sweet yellow sauce **which** the British put on puddings. And you were right – tea with milk is absolutely disgusting!

I'm sending some photos **which** I took with my new camera – hope you like them!

I'm going back to Rotterdam for a few days at Christmas. I hope you can come and visit me this time.

Best wishes,
Sanne XX

PS. The Colliers have a rabbit called Robbie **that** sleeps in a little bed in the kitchen! See the photo.

Work it out

3 Look at Sanne's email again and answer the questions.

Which of the words in bold is referring to:
a people? _____ and _____
b possessions? _____
c objects or things? _____ and _____
d places? _____

4 Look at sentences 1 and 2. Then circle the correct answer to the rule, a or b.

1 One thing (that) I really love here is custard. It's a sweet yellow sauce (which) the British put on puddings.
2 Everyone that lives here is an actor or a rock star.

We can leave out *who/which/that* when they are followed by:
a a pronoun (a word like *you, she, everybody*) or a noun.
b a verb.

Check it out

Relative pronouns

Who and *that* refer to people.
Everyone **that** lives here is an actor or a rock star.
Charles has got a lot of little friends **who** come to play with him.

Which and *that* refer to objects and things.
I'm sending some photos **which** I took with my new camera.
One thing **that** I really love here is custard.

Whose refers to possessions.
They're the couple **whose** son I'm looking after.

Where refers to places.
It's a place **where** a lot of rich people live.

We can leave out *who/which/that* when they are followed by a noun or a pronoun.
One thing I like is custard. = One thing **that** I like is custard.

44

5 Circle the correct relative pronouns. Sometimes more than one answer is possible. Tick the sentences where you can leave out *who, which* or *that*.

1 That's the boy *that / who / which* delivers our newspapers. ☐
2 This is the key *which / who / where* you need to open the back door. ☐
3 This is the room *which / where / that* you're sleeping tonight. ☐
4 That's the house *that / which / whose* I was telling you about. ☐
5 That's the man *whose / who / that* daughter I went to school with. ☐
6 The man *which / whose / who* you saw is a gardener. ☐
7 The new car *that / which / whose* we bought last year was very expensive. ☐

6 CD 2.1 Listen and complete the plan of the Colliers' house.

kitchen   dining room   bathroom
cupboard   bedroom

GROUND FLOOR

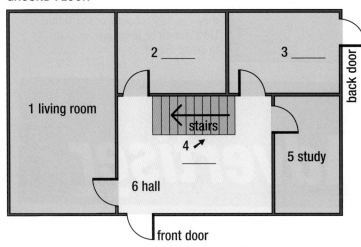

FIRST FLOOR

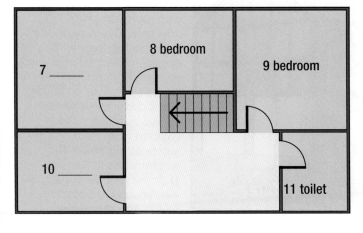

7 CD 2.1 Listen again and look at the plan. In which rooms can you find these things? Write the numbers.

TV ☐   shower ☐   computer ☐
wardrobe ☐   DVD player ☐   desk ☐
freezer ☐   washing machine ☐
vacuum cleaner ☐

8 CD 2.2 Write the missing relative pronouns. Listen and check.

1 This is the computer _____ he writes his reports on.
2 The money on the table is for the man _____ is coming to fix the washing machine tomorrow morning.
3 There's a cupboard in the hall _____ we keep the vacuum cleaner.
4 I used to work with a woman _____ husband was a brilliant artist.
5 He asked us to choose the pictures _____ we liked best.

9 CD 2.2 Circle the relative pronouns in Exercise 8 which can be left out. Then listen and check.

10 Match 1–6 with a–f to make sentences.

1 A washing machine is a thing ☐
2 A living room is a place ☐
3 A dining room is a place ☐
4 A dustbin is a place ☐
5 A remote control is a thing ☐

a where you put rubbish.
b that you use to change TV channels.
c that you use to wash clothes.
d where people relax in the evenings.
e where you eat.

11 Now write definitions for the things below. Use the verbs in the box.

clean   look after   deliver   boil   keep

1 A postman is a person *who delivers letters*.
2 A kettle is a thing _____ .
3 A garage is a place _____ .
4 A vacuum cleaner is a thing _____ .
5 A childminder is a person _____ .

12 Complete the sentences for you.

1 _____ is the room where I spend most of my time.
2 _____ is the place where I usually spend Saturday evenings.
3 _____ is the person who I trust the most.
4 _____ is the possession which is most important to me.

The Daily Post

May 31 1956

The future is here today?

The 1956 Ideal Home Exhibition opened yesterday in London. Perhaps the most interesting display is The House of the Future – a vision of life at the end of the twentieth century. All the walls inside and outside the house are plastic. There is an exotic garden inside the house. The public also have a chance to see some gadgets from the future. There is a remote control for the lights and the enormous television set (it has a twelve-inch screen!) There is a gadget which cleans the bath every time you use it. A special button hides the tables in the floor when you are not using them. Many people are already asking how they can buy a house of the future. Unfortunately, there are no plans to build them!

Ⓑ **The Lowestoft Advertiser**

May 2005

The Intelligent House

A This is the 'intelligent' house [1] _____ nearly everything and makes everyday life much easier. From the outside it looks like an average detached house – the furniture, TV and fridge are the same as in any other home. But this house is full of surprises.

B The intelligent house has many innovations. A computer controls the heating and the lighting. If you're at work and the computer decides the house isn't warm enough, it switches on the heating. It can prepare coffee for you as you're watching your favourite TV programme. Cameras, [2] _____, keep an eye on the children upstairs when you are in the garden or even at the office. The house even knows what is in your fridge and can make a shopping list for you.

C The computer works outside the house, too. When you come home from the supermarket, a camera above the door 'sees' your heavy bags of shopping and opens the door for you. You can see anybody [3] _____ without leaving your armchair. The cameras are linked to the Internet so you can even check what is going on outside your house when you're at work or on holiday – just check the house's special web page. The computer can even automatically water the garden when it's too dry.

D A vision of the future? No – companies are building houses like this at the moment. And who are these houses for? The companies believe these houses are ideal for busy people [4] _____. But there is one small problem – a house like this costs over £700,000!

READING

1 Read text A and look at the photo. Answer the questions.

1 When was this house displayed?
2 Does The House of the Future look modern today?
3 In your opinion, is the house a comfortable place to live?
4 In your opinion, what is the most unusual thing in it?
5 Did any of the architects' ideas about the future really happen?

2 Read text B and match subjects 1–5 with paragraphs A–D. There is one extra heading.

1 The future is here today ☐
2 The history of the intelligent house ☐
3 Inside the intelligent house ☐
4 What is an 'intelligent' house? ☐
5 How technology helps outside the house ☐

3 [CD 2.3] Read text B again and complete it with sentences a–d. Then listen and check.

a that comes to your door
b where technology controls
c which are in every bedroom
d whose jobs require a lot of travel

4 Look at the texts again and decide which house the sentences describe, A or B. There are two sentences which describe both houses.

1 This house can open the front door for you.
2 This house can clean the bath for you.
3 You don't have to go outside to water the garden.
4 The outside of the house is not very unusual.
5 This house has some unusual furniture.
6 It is easy to control the lights in this house.

5 Work in groups. Which of these things would/wouldn't you like to have in your home? Why?/Why not?

- a bath that cleans itself
- lights you control with a remote control
- a camera that tells you who's at the front door
- a washing machine that finds lost socks
- cameras which show you what is happening in all the bedrooms
- a fridge that makes its own shopping list
- a bedroom door that can be programmed to keep out brothers/sisters/parents
- an alarm clock that understands your commands

I would like to have a bath that cleans itself, because I'm very lazy!

VOCABULARY

1 Think Back! Put these words into the table. In groups, add other words to each category.

armchair drive hall study attic
DVD player kettle TV freezer kitchen
vacuum cleaner toilet video cupboard
bathroom garage living room wardrobe
statue fountain porch dining room
garden sofa washing machine balcony

Rooms/places in the house	Furniture	Appliances	Things outside the house
hall	armchair	DVD player	drive

2 Check the meaning of the new words and put them in the table in Exercise 1.

basement stairs bookshelf heater
chest of drawers microwave doorbell
letter box lawn

3 Do these adjectives have a positive (+) or a negative (–) meaning? Use a dictionary to help you. Some words have a positive and a negative meaning.

Adjectives to describe homes
bright cosy original roomy tasteless
expensive spacious elegant ugly attractive
comfortable tiny modern tasteful uncomfortable

4 [CD 2.4] Read the text on page 140 and choose the correct words. Then listen and check. What kind of room is the person describing?

5 Write a description of your bedroom. Look at the text on page 140 to help you. Include the following information.

Paragraph 1
1 Do you like it? Why?/Why not?
2 Is the room big/comfortable/warm/ sunny (enough)?
3 What can you see from the window?

Paragraph 2
1 Do you have any decorations like pictures or posters on the wall/door?
2 What kind of furniture/appliances have you got in the room?

SPEAKING

1 In pairs, look at the pictures and answer the questions.

- What type of accommodation does each picture show? Choose from the ideas below.

....

a semi-detached house   terraced houses   a villa
a cottage   a block of flats   a detached house

....

- What type of accommodation do you think is:
  - the most attractive?
  - the most modern?
  - the most comfortable?
- What kind of accommodation is most common in your country?
- What kind of home does your family live in?

2 **CD 2.5** Listen and decide which picture in Exercise 1 the speaker is describing.

3 Read the description on page 140 and answer the questions.

1 What does the speaker talk about first – small details or a summary of what the picture shows?
2 Which tense does the speaker use to describe actions?
3 Which phrases does the speaker use to describe where something is in the picture?
4 Does the speaker have a negative or a positive reaction to the picture? Why?

4 Study Speak Out and check your answers to Exercise 3.

SPEAK OUT | Describing pictures

Start by saying what the picture shows in general.
The picture shows a street of terraced houses in a city.

Use the Present Continuous to describe what people are doing.
There are two old men on the right who **are chatting**.

Talk about what you can see in more detail. Use the following phrases to describe where things are:

**in the background/middle/foreground
at the bottom/top
on the right/left**

There's somebody washing his car **in the background**.

Use phrases like *perhaps* and *(it) might be* if you are making a guess.
It might be in Britain.
Perhaps it's in Germany.

Use *it looks* + adjective to show how you feel about the picture.
It looks **very friendly**.

---

5 Look at picture 3. What does the picture show in general?

3

6 CD 2.6 Look at picture 3 again and complete the missing phrases. Then listen and check.

1 _____ of the picture some children are playing.
2 _____ some elderly people are sitting on a bench and talking.
3 _____ somebody is reading.
4 _____ a woman is walking with a bag.

Mind the trap!

Usually when we describe what we can see in general we use the words *a* and *some*.

On the right **a** woman is talking on **a** mobile phone. There are **some** cars and **a** bus in the background.

But when we talk about something for the second time we use *the*.
There's **a** small cottage in the background. **The** cottage looks very attractive.

---

7 What else can you say about picture 3? Answer the questions.

1 Can you guess which country or place the people are in? Why do you think so?
2 Which adjectives describe the scene best? Choose three from the list.

attractive bright pleasant nice relaxed
boring colourful horrible quiet ugly

8 Look at picture 1 and follow the instructions.

• Look at Speak Out and make notes on what you are going to say. Use the text on page 140 to help you.
• Describe the picture to your partner.

9 Choose one of the pictures above and describe it to your partner.

10 Complete the sentences to make them true about a typical home in your country. Then compare your answers with a partner.

1 People in my country usually live in a _____ .
2 The typical home has got _____ bedrooms.
3 Most homes are rather _____ and _____ .
4 Most people _____ a garage.
5 Nearly everybody has got a TV, a _____ and a _____ .

Eat up!

Read, listen and talk about food; diets; lifestyles.
Practise countable and uncountable nouns; quantifiers.
Focus on complaining and apologising; food and diets vocabulary.
Write a questionnaire.

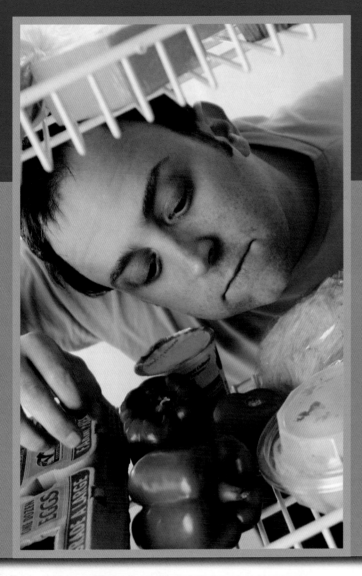

You are what you eat!

The inside of your fridge says a lot about you: not only your diet but your lifestyle, personality and attitude to life too. *Your Home* asked food expert Marcus Laroche to look inside the fridges of three of our readers.

A There is **not much** <u>food</u> here but I can see that food is very important to the owner of this fridge. This person looks after his/her health and has a balanced diet with fresh <u>fruit</u> and **a lot of** <u>vegetables</u>. There's a lot of mineral water – very healthy! The food is not only healthy, but looks good too – I can see avocados, **some** <u>red peppers</u>, **a few** <u>grapes</u> and a melon. Perhaps this person is a vegan – I ca**n't** see **any** <u>milk</u> or <u>cheese</u>. I'm sure he/she has a healthy body and a tasteful home too!

B This fridge is a mess – there is simply **too much** <u>food</u> in here! This person obviously loves cooking – there isn't any convenience food here. And he/she has got a very big appetite and probably doesn't know what a diet is. Look at all those eggs and sausages! There's a lot to drink too: **some** <u>wine</u>, beer and **a lot of** <u>fruit juice</u>. My guess is that this person loves food but isn't terribly healthy!

C This person obviously only eats to live. There are**n't many** <u>things</u> in this fridge – it's the classic minimalist fridge! There's a tub of margarine, a bar of chocolate and **a little** <u>chocolate cake</u>. This person certainly has a sweet tooth! I ca**n't** see **any** <u>vegetables</u> or fresh fruit. What a terrible diet! I'm afraid this person is probably very lazy and doesn't cook at all – he/she probably doesn't enjoy life very much!

GRAMMAR AND VOCABULARY

1 Put the words in the right category. Use a dictionary if you need to. Then work in groups and add other words for each category.

> avocado   chocolate   chocolate cake   melon
> red pepper   beer   eggs   grapes   milk
> sausages   cheese   cabbage   yoghurt   ham
> chicken   broccoli   fruit juice   ice cream
> mineral water   wine   salmon   pizza   tomato
> tuna   bread

Fruit/Vegetables	Meat/Fish	Dairy	Drinks	Other
avocado	sausages	eggs	fruit juice	pizza

2 In groups, discuss which things in Exercise 1 you like and dislike the most. Find out who has the most similar likes and dislikes to you.

3 **CD 2.7** Read the descriptions A–C. In pairs, decide who owns each fridge. Then listen and check.

> *I think a doctor owns fridge A because the food looks very healthy.*

- a family with teenage kids ☐
- a yoga instructor ☐
- a businessman ☐
- a student ☐
- a doctor ☐

50

Work it out

4 Look at the article again and answer the questions.

   1 Which of the <u>underlined</u> nouns are uncountable? Circle them.

   2 Can these nouns be plural?

5 Look at the words in bold in the article and answer the questions.

   1 Which of these words or phrases are used with both countable and uncountable nouns?

   2 Which of these words or phrases are only used with uncountable nouns?

   3 Which of these words or phrases are only used with countable nouns?

   4 Which two phrases mean *some but not a lot*?

Check it out

Quantifiers	
Countable nouns	
Are there **any** eggs? **How many** eggs are there?	
There are **too many** There are **a lot of** There are **some** There are**n't many**/There are **a few** There are**n't any**	eggs.
Uncountable nouns	
Is there **any** cheese? **How much** cheese is there?	
There is **too much** There is **a lot of** There is **some** There is**n't much** /There is **a little** There is**n't any**	cheese.

6 Circle the correct words.

   1 How *much / many* bananas did you buy?

   2 We need *some / any* butter.

   3 Are there *any / some* spoons in the drawer?

   4 Don't put too *much / many* water in the kettle!

   5 You didn't buy *any / some* sausages.

   6 Is there *some / any* rice left?

   7 She doesn't eat *a lot of / many* meat.

   8 Can I have *a little / a few* milk, please?

   9 He eats *too much / a lot of* sweets every day.

7 In pairs, look at the photo below. Write sentences using these words and phrases.

crisps salad peanuts bread olives
orange juice cheese grapes biscuits

There is a lot of/a little ...
There are some/a few/a lot of ...
There aren't many/any ...
There isn't much ...
There is a jar/carton of ....

There's a lot of salad.

8 In groups, find out about each other's diets. Use the prompts below and make notes.

In your group who has:
- the healthiest diet?
- the biggest appetite?
- the sweetest tooth?

A *How much fruit/convenience food do you eat?*
B *I eat too much/too many/a lot of/a little/ a few ... .*

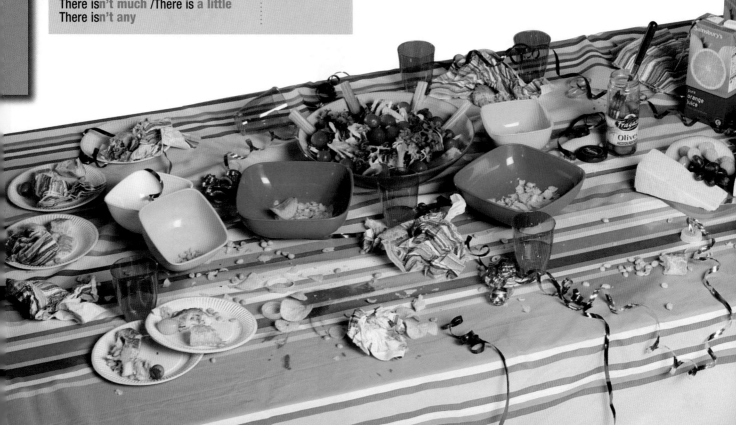

READING AND LISTENING

1 In pairs, look at the pictures and answer the questions.

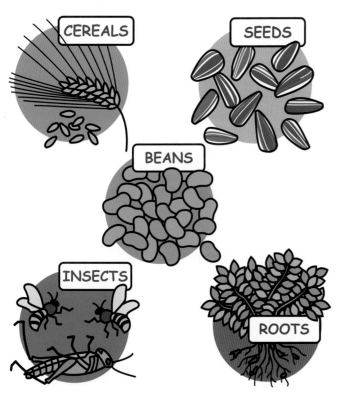

CEREALS

SEEDS

BEANS

INSECTS

ROOTS

- Which of these things are a part of people's diets in your country?
- Which of these things would you not like to try?

2 Read the text opposite quickly and decide which sentence is the best summary of the article.

1 People in Europe only started to eat meat during the nineteenth century.
2 Most people in the western world eat more meat today than their ancestors.
3 In many countries people don't eat meat.

3 Read the paragraphs below and decide which one is the missing second paragraph from the article.

A Today many famous sportsmen and models choose not to eat meat. Brad Pitt, Liv Tyler, Kim Basinger and Michael J. Fox are just a few examples of film stars who are vegetarian. We can add a lot of rock and pop stars to the list too: Bob Dylan, rapper Dr Dre, Krist Novoselic of Nirvana, Mel C, Peter Gabriel, Prince, Moby and Robert Smith of The Cure all refuse to eat meat.

B How do we know? One important clue is our teeth. Just like animals which eat plants, humans have teeth called molars (these are the large, flat teeth at the back of our mouths) which we need to break down hard food such as seeds. Archaeologists can also tell us about diets of the past. In fact, we know a lot about the human diet over the last 7,000 years.

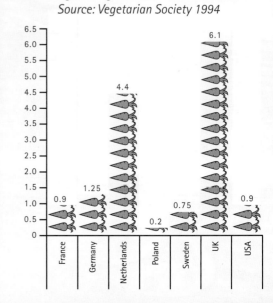

Percentage of vegetarians in various countries
Source: Vegetarian Society 1994

Country	Percentage
France	0.9
Germany	1.25
Netherlands	4.4
Poland	0.2
Sweden	0.75
UK	6.1
USA	0.9

Was Fred Flintstone a vegetarian?

Some anthropologists now think that for millions of years man's diet was more than 80 percent vegetarian. Alan Vega investigates ...

Twenty-four million years ago when our ancestors lived in the tropical forests of central Africa, they probably ate plants and fruit, and from time to time a few insects. When these prehistoric people started to travel north into the savannah their diet changed too, and they began to eat a lot of seeds and other plant material. And this is probably how man lived for the next twenty-two million years, eating roots, seeds, fruit, nuts, vegetables and occasionally a little meat.

The Aztecs and Incas ate a lot of cereals, beans and fruit and not much meat at all. In classical India most people didn't eat meat and the Japanese were mainly vegetarian until a few generations ago. The main food of the slaves who built the Pyramids was boiled onions! Even today, some societies whose lifestyles are unchanged (like the Aborigines of Western Australia) are still mostly vegetarian.

During the nineteenth century people in western countries suddenly began to eat a lot more meat. New methods of keeping and killing animals, better transport and new inventions like fridges and freezers helped to reduce the price of meat for ordinary people. It was probably at this time that the typical western meal that millions of people eat every day – meat, potatoes and vegetables – was born.

Also during the nineteenth century, the vegetarian movement started in Europe and the USA. But it was only in the 1960s that more and more people in the west decided to give up meat in their diets. So why do people choose to be vegetarian? Many people decide to become vegetarian for personal reasons. First of all, some people think that it is healthier not to eat meat. Others believe that it is cruel to eat animals. The Irish writer George Bernard Shaw once said, 'Animals are my friends – and I don't eat my friends'. Finally there are some people who think that growing food for cows and pigs to eat is not very economical. Today vegetarianism is more and more popular in Europe and the USA. But in most countries people who never eat meat are still a very small minority.

---

4 CD ROM **Read the article again and circle the best answer.**

1 Millions of years ago our ancestors
  a moved from the savannah to central Africa.
  b didn't eat much meat.
  c mostly ate insects.

2 The Japanese
  a used to eat meat but stopped.
  b have the same diet as people in classical India.
  c didn't eat much meat until recently.

3 In the nineteenth century people started eating more meat because
  a a lot of people bought fridges and freezers.
  b it was popular to eat the same things every day.
  c technology helped the price of meat to fall.

4 In the 1960s
  a the vegetarian movement was born in Europe and the USA.
  b a lot of people decided to go on a diet.
  c many people stopped eating meat.

5 George Bernard Shaw didn't eat meat because
  a he thought that it was unkind to kill animals.
  b he wanted to do the same as his friends.
  c he wanted to keep healthy.

6 In the western world today
  a vegetarianism is growing all the time.
  b there are more vegetarians than people who eat meat.
  c vegetarianism is less common than in the 1960s.

5 CD 2.8 **Check any new words in the diets a–d. Then listen and match the speakers with their diet.**

Naomi ☐   Rob ☐   Will ☐   Sue ☐

a vegetarian
b only eats white meat (turkey, chicken) and fish
c vegan (no meat or animal products)
d loves red meat (beef and lamb)

6 CD 2.8 **Read statements 1–8. Then listen again and match them with the speakers.**

Naomi ☐☐   Rob ☐☐   Will ☐☐   Sue ☐☐

1 I love dishes with chicken.
2 Killing animals is wrong.
3 It's quite difficult to find vegetarian/vegan products in the shops.
4 I used to eat a lot of meat but I eat less now.
5 Meat is tasty and it's good for you.
6 Some people think people who don't eat meat get ill easily.
7 Vegetarian food isn't very filling.
8 It's against my religion to eat meat.

7 **Are you a vegetarian? Why?/Why not? Discuss in groups. Use the statements from Exercise 6 to help you.**

A

B   Fast food restaurant

Restaurant

C   Pizzeria

VOCABULARY

1 In pairs, look at the photos and answer the questions.

Where is the best place to:
1 have a snack between classes?
2 eat out with friends after watching a film?
3 take somebody on a romantic first date?

2 (CD 2.9) Use a dictionary to check these words. Listen and tick the words you hear.

a burger and milkshake ☐   a sandwich ☐
a cream cake ☐   goulash ☐   lasagne ☐
apple pie and ice cream ☐   steak and chips ☐
pizza ☐   garlic bread ☐   salad ☐
chocolate cake ☐   fish and chips ☐
chicken curry with rice ☐   tomato soup ☐
spaghetti bolognaise ☐   cappuccino ☐

3 (CD 2.9) Listen again and look at the photos. Which places are the people talking about?

1 ☐   2 ☐   3 ☐

4 In pairs, look at the list in Exercise 2 again and answer the questions.

1 Which food do you eat for starters/desserts/main courses?
2 Which food is suitable for vegetarians?

5 Match words 1–6 with their opposite meanings a–f. Use a dictionary if you need to.

1 sweet	☐	a unhealthy
2 spicy	☐	b stale
3 low fat	☐	c tasteless
4 healthy	☐	d mild
5 delicious	☐	e bitter
6 fresh	☐	f greasy

> **TRAIN YOUR BRAIN | Dictionary skills**
>
> **Word stress**
> If you are unsure about which syllable has the main stress, a dictionary can help you. The ' symbol comes before the syllable with the main stress.
>
> **café** /'kæfeɪ/ **n** [C] **1** a small restaurant where you can buy drinks and simple meals.

6 Use a dictionary and mark the main stress in these words. Then practise saying them.

kebab   lemonade   margarine   menu   pizza
carton   avocado   dessert   recipe   melon

SPEAKING

1 In pairs, look at the picture. Do you think this is a good place to eat out? Why?/Why not?

2 Match sentences a–e with speech bubbles 1–5 in the picture.

a The music's too loud! ☐
b It isn't hot enough. And what is this doing here? ☐
c It's the wrong order! We didn't ask for this! ☐
d Ow! ☐
e There's a mistake in the bill! ☐

3 **CD 2.10** Study Speak Out. Then listen and tick the apologies you hear.

SPEAK OUT | Complaining and apologising

Complaining	Apologising
Excuse me,/I'm sorry but, ...	**I'm (really) sorry, ...**
it's very/too	about that.
it isn't ... enough./It isn't very	I didn't mean to ... .
it isn't working properly.	it was an accident.
there's a mistake (in the bill/order).	I completely forgot.
it's the wrong order.	it was rather stupid of me.
you forgot to	I didn't realise.
	I ... by mistake.

Mind the trap!

If somebody apologises to you first, it is polite to accept their apology.
I'm sorry I'm late. **Never mind.**
Oh! I'm really sorry. It was an accident. **That's OK!**

4 In pairs, write a complaint for each situation. Use Speak Out to help you.

1 You lent your friend your MP3 player. He gave it back and now it doesn't play.
   I'm sorry, but my MP3 player isn't working properly.
2 Your neighbours are having a party. It's noisy and you can't sleep.
3 Your friend was supposed to phone you. You waited all day but he didn't phone.
4 You bought a sandwich. The bread is very stale.
5 You ordered a ham and mushroom pizza. The waitress brings you a tuna and pineapple pizza.

5 Match your complaints (1–5) from Exercise 4 with the apologies a–e. Then practise the dialogues in pairs.

a I'm very sorry about your order. It was very careless of me. ☐
b I'm sorry – it wasn't my fault. My brother was on the phone all evening. ☐
c I'm sorry. I dropped it – it was an accident! ☐
d I'm sorry about the noise. I didn't realise. ☐
e I'm very sorry. I gave you an old one by mistake. ☐

6 In pairs, write a short dialogue for these situations. Then practise your dialogues.

1 You bought a hotdog from the college canteen. It isn't very hot and there's no ketchup in it.
2 You borrowed a CD from a friend. You dropped it and now it doesn't play.

WRITING

1 In pairs, look at questionnaire A and answer the questions.

1 What do you think the purpose of the questionnaire is?
2 What do you think *M/F* and *Y/N* mean?
3 Is Jodie happy with the service in the supermarket? How do you know?

2 Study Train Your Brain and look at questionnaire B. Can you find any mistakes or problems in the questionnaire?

TRAIN YOUR BRAIN | Questionnaires

1 Give your questionnaire a title so it's clear what it is for.
2 Make sure you only ask for information you really need.
3 Make sure each question only asks about one thing.
4 Write your questions in a logical order – personal information like name or age should be together at the top. Be careful with word order!
5 Check that any multiple choice questions include all the possible answers.

---

3 Match questions 1–4 with the groups of answers a–d below.

1 How often do you buy *Top One* magazine? ☐
2 Are you happy with the service in our restaurants? ☐
3 How do you find the prices in our snack bar? ☐
4 What do you think about the choice of goods in our supermarket? ☐

a cheap / average / _____
b _____ / average / good
c unhappy / _____ / very satisfied
d never / sometimes / _____

4 Complete each group of answers a–d in Exercise 3 with words from the box.

....
expensive   often   poor   quite satisfied
....

NOW EVEN MORE TOMATOES!

BEST TASTE EVER!

56

A

Micro Supermarkets PLC
Customer Satisfaction Questionnaire

MICRO SUPERMARKETS · LOW PRICES ·

* please circle your choice as required

First name   Jodie

Surname   Mellors

M (F)

Age*
under 25   (25–35)   35–55   55+

Daytime telephone number   392345

Do you have a car?* (Y) N

How often do you shop at Micro each month?
once a week

Which of these things do you usually buy at Micro?*
(fruit and vegetables) meat (bread and rolls)
cosmetics (soft drinks) alcohol

How expensive do you find our products?*
cheap (average) expensive

Are you happy with our service?*
yes (quite happy) unhappy

Are you happy with the range of products on offer?
I'd like to see a better choice of vegetarian food.

How can Micro improve its service?
Perhaps you could open longer in the evenings.

Thank you for your time!

5 Write the words and phrases in the correct order to make questions. Then match them with answers a–f.

1 how often/do/our restaurant/visit/you?

_____ ☐

2 the service/you/satisfied with/are?

_____ ☐

3 buy/you/in our shop/what/usually/do?

_____ ☐

4 in our café/do/think of/the prices/you/what?

_____ ☐

5 your/what/the new menu/is/opinion of?

_____ ☐

6 improve/can/our service/we/how?

_____ ☐

a Quite expensive
b You should open on Sundays too.
c CDs and books
d Yes, very satisfied
e It's better than before.
f About twice a week

6 In groups, write a customer satisfaction questionnaire for your school snack bar or canteen. Use the information below and Train Your Brain to help you write questions.

1 What personal information do you need to know about your customers? Name/Age/Class/Gender/Phone number?
2 Which of these things do you want to ask about in your questionnaire? Choose at least four.

- prices
- service
- choice
- opening hours
- quality of the food
- what you usually buy
- how often you visit
- how to improve service

Metro-Comecon
HOTELS PLC

First name _____

Gender   Male ◯   Female ◯

Age

under 15 ◯   17–25 ◯   45–55 ◯   55+ ◯   25–35 ◯

Do you find our prices

😃 Cheap   😐 Average   🙂 Not expensive

Is this your first stay in this hotel?

Yes ◯   No ◯

Weight (kg) _____

Shoe size _____

Surname _____

How clean and how comfortable do you find our hotel?

😐 Average   🙂 Good   😄 Very good

How can Metro-Comecon improve its service?

_____
_____
_____
_____
_____

Please turn over ➡

NEW IMPROVED RECIPE!

LESS DISGUSTING TASTE!

TOTALLY INEDIBLE!

VOCABULARY AND GRAMMAR

1 Complete the crossword puzzle and find the secret message.

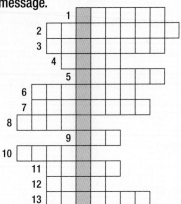

1 It uses electricity and keeps you warm.
2 A place for your books.
3 A comfortable chair.
4 You do your homework on it.
5 It's quicker than a bath.
6 I keep my clothes in a chest of … .
7 A room at the bottom of the house.
8 Between the street and the garage.
9 You turn it on and water comes out.
10 A covered space at the front door.
11 The thing that you walk on.
12 It gives you light.
13 This is where you can find ice cream.

2 Look at the food items in the box and answer the questions. Some items can be used more than once.

apple pie banana beef beer butter
cabbage cheese chicken chips tuna
chocolate coffee crisps garlic ham
ice cream mushrooms onion yoghurt
orange juice pork salad sausages tea

Which food items:
1 are drinks? _____ , _____ , _____ ,

_____

2 can vegetarians not eat? _____ ,

_____ , _____ , _____ , _____ ,

_____

3 are vegetables?_____ , _____ ,

_____ , _____ , _____

4 are sweet? _____ , _____ , _____ ,

_____

5 come from potatoes? _____ , _____

6 are milk products? _____ , _____ ,

_____ ,

3 Complete the tables with the adjectives in the box.

bitter bright cosy delicious dull tiny
filling fresh greasy quiet roomy stale
sweet tasteful tasty uncomfortable

Homes		Food	
Positive	Negative	Positive	Negative
bright			

4 Complete the second sentence so that it has a similar meaning to the first sentence. Use the word in bold and other words to complete each sentence.

1 I haven't had a worse day in my life. **the**
It was _____ of my life.
2 Maggie is prettier than Kate. **as**
Kate _____ Maggie.
3 There's only a little money in the drawer.
much
There _____ in the drawer.
4 My flat isn't big enough to invite people for dinner. **small**
My flat _____ to invite people for dinner.
5 There isn't one café in this part of town. **any**
There _____ in this part of town.

5 Complete the text. For each gap circle the correct answer.

Windsor is the ¹___ inhabited castle in the world with nearly 1,000 years of royal history. Today, it is one of the Queen's official homes. When she is staying at the castle, there is a flag ²___ flies above the White Tower.

In 1992, there was a terrible fire ³___ destroyed more than 100 rooms in the castle. However, only five years later the castle was open to the public again – and it was just ⁴___ beautiful as before.

Windsor is one of ⁵___ popular tourist attractions in the UK. There are about one million people ⁶___ visit it each year because there is so ⁷___ to see there. Only the Tower of London and Edinburgh Castle receive ⁸___ visitors than Windsor Castle. There is a website ⁹___ you can buy tickets, and when you get to the Castle, there are many guides ¹⁰___ job it is to explain the fascinating history of this marvellous castle.

1 a largest	**b** larger	**c** large
2 a who	**b** which	**c** whose
3 a where	**b** whose	**c** which
4 a as	**b** more	**c** most
5 a more	**b** most	**c** the most
6 a which	**b** whose	**c** who
7 a more	**b** most	**c** much
8 a more	**b** most	**c** much
9 a where	**b** whose	**c** which
10 a where	**b** whose	**c** which

PRONUNCIATION

1 〔CD 2.11〕 Listen to the words and circle the sounds that you don't hear. Then listen again and repeat.

answer business cupboard daughter
every half grandmother island lamb
neighbour sandwich Wednesday

58

READING SKILLS

1 Read the letter. Tick true and cross false.

Toledo, Ohio
23 January

Re: *Cheese in a Tube* TV commercial

Dear Sir/Madam,

I am writing to complain about the TV commercial for your product *Cheese in a Tube*. In my opinion, there is some false information in the commercial, and it also encourages children to adopt bad eating habits.

In the commercial, there is a popular TV cartoon character who says that *Cheese in a Tube* is 'the best cheese in the world'. This is obviously not true. However, I have two young children who love the cartoon character in the commercial. So now they believe that your cheese is the best in the world and they don't want any other kind.

The cartoon character then says that *Cheese in a Tube* is 'good for young kids'. Well, I checked the information on the packet. There certainly isn't very much cheese in your product – only 5% – and it has more calories and fat than chocolate! It's probably one of the unhealthiest things you can buy in the supermarket. Child obesity is a huge problem in our country. Our children are the fattest and unhealthiest in the world, and products like yours just make things worse.

Finally, the commercial ends with two beautiful, slim, healthy-looking children sitting in front of the TV. Their mother calls them to come to the kitchen to eat a nutritious salad. The children say they're watching their favourite cartoon – the same character who is in the commercial, of course – so what does the mother do? She brings each of them some *Cheese in a Tube*! The parents eat their salad in the kitchen while the children suck their lunch from a tube in front of the TV! I believe that it's good for children and parents to eat together, but obviously your company doesn't.

Please change this terrible commercial. And why don't you start making healthier foods too?

Yours sincerely,

Maddy Moore

Maddy Moore

1 Maddy Moore is writing to a TV company. ☐
2 Maddy's children believe what the cartoon character tells them. ☐
3 *Cheese in a Tube* is healthier than chocolate. ☐
4 Maddy thinks that there are a lot of fat children in her country. ☐
5 The commercial shows a family enjoying a meal together. ☐
6 Maddy wants the company to stop showing the commercial. ☐

SPEAKING SKILLS

1 Roleplay the conversation.

Student A
You are in an English restaurant, unhappy with the meal you ordered. Talk to the waiter/waitress.
• Say how disappointed you are, giving at least two reasons.
• Ask what the waiter/waitress is going to do about it.
• Accept the suggested solution.
You start the conversation.

Student B
You are a waiter/waitress in an English restaurant. Your client is disappointed with the meal s/he ordered.
• Say you are sorry that your client is disappointed with the dish s/he ordered.
• Apologise for the situation, saying why it happened.
• Suggest a good solution.
Your partner starts the conversation.

2 Describe the photo. Then answer the questions.

1 What do you think the people in the photo are celebrating? Why?
2 Would you like to go to a very formal dinner like this? Why?/Why not?

Look to the future

Read, listen and talk about future predictions; technology; the environment.
Practise *going to* and *will* for predictions; first conditional.
Focus on probability and inference; listening for specific information.
Write a campaign leaflet.

GRAMMAR AND LISTENING

1 Look at the photos and read the captions. Is Luke optimistic or pessimistic about June 13, the day of his Maths exam?

'I'm going to be late for my exam. It's going to be another terrible day.'

'Oh no! It's going to rain.'

'I don't know any of the answers. I'm not going to pass.'

2 Match texts A–C with text types 1–3 below. Are they optimistic or pessimistic?

1 A horoscope ☐
2 A school report ☐
3 A weather forecast ☐

A
Friday June 13
After a cloudy start, it will be dry and warm. Temperatures 24–26°C.

B
GEMINI – May 22–June 21
Friday will be a day of pleasant surprises. With Pluto around, you'll want to slow down and enjoy yourself!

C
Maths 1B Luke won't have any problems in passing his Maths exam in June, but he has to believe in himself more! J Barnard

French 2A Luke is working hard and is making good progress. A Thorpe

Work it out

3 Match sentences 1–2 with definitions a–b.

1 Look at the clouds. It's going to rain.
2 I am confident that Luke will pass his exam in June.

a An opinion, belief or guess about the future
b A confident prediction about the future when we can see now what is certain to happen next

4 Look at these sentences from the photos. Match Luke's predictions 1–4 with the evidence he uses a–d.

1 It's going to rain. ☐
2 It's going to be another terrible day! ☐
3 I'm going to be late for my exam. ☐
4 I'm not going to pass! ☐

a I'm having a really bad day!
b I don't know any of the answers!
c I can see dark clouds!
d It's nine o'clock!

Check it out

Future predictions

We use *going to* and *will* to talk about future predictions.

We use *going to* when we can see (or hear) now what is certain to happen next and so we are quite sure about our prediction.

I'm not going to pass this exam. (I don't know any of these answers!)
Oh no! It's going to rain. (I can see the clouds.)

We use *will/won't* for what we believe will happen in the future. Often we are only guessing.

The forecast says it won't rain at the weekend.
Don't worry. I'm sure you'll find a job soon.

5 Read the situations and write a sentence with *going to*. Use the verbs below.

miss   fall   faint   be (x2)   crash

1 The train is very crowded and it's very hot. Megan is looking very pale. She's going to faint .
2 Jackie starts school at 9.00. It's 8.50 and she's still washing her hair. She _____ late.
3 The road is very wet and the man is driving too fast. He _____ .
4 Philip's running to the bus stop. His shoelaces are undone. He _____ .
5 Tom's train is leaving at 7.30. It's 7.28 and he's queuing for his ticket. He _____ his train.
6 There's a terrible mess in the kitchen. My parents are coming home in a few minutes. They _____ very angry.

6 Circle the correct answers.

1 Experts believe that, in 2030, the world's population *will / is going to* be eight billion.
2 The coach is very hot and crowded. It *will / is going to* be a very uncomfortable journey!
3 That waiter is carrying too much. He *will / is going to* drop those glasses!
4 I think that travelling by plane *will / is going to* be cheaper in the future.
5 Do you think that people *will / are going to* live on the Moon in the future?
6 It's getting colder and colder. It *will / is going to* snow tonight.

7 [CD 2.12] Listen to the fortune teller and look at her predictions. In groups, try and guess what will happen in Eve's life.

YOU WILL BE IN A PLACE WITH A LOT OF WATER.

SOMEBODY FROM BELOW WILL ASK YOU FOR HELP.

THERE'S A TALL YOUNG MAN WHO YOU'LL BE VERY PLEASED TO SEE.

HE WILL ONLY BE INTERESTED IN YOUR MONEY.

A I think she'll go to the seaside.
B I think a man will rescue her at the swimming pool.

8 [CD 2.13] Listen to the end of the story. Were any of your predictions correct? What was the explanation for things 1–3?

1 the place with a lot of water
2 the person from below
3 the man interested in the money

Back   Forward   Stop   Refresh   Home   AutoFill   Print   Mail

Address: @ www1.looktothefuture.co.uk

Favorites   History   Search   Scrapbook   Page Holder

Technology | Look To The Future

Home   Internet links   Research   Contac

The Fruits of Technology

Look To The Future asked our team of experts to make four predictions for the next twenty years.

1 The Internet

Experts all agree that in the near future the Internet will become more and more important. The most exciting changes will probably be in education. It's possible that in the future each pupil will have a laptop - there probably won't be paper or textbooks in thirty years and computers will certainly be cheaper! Students will go on day trips with their class to the Louvre in France or visit the Arctic Tundra - all by Internet and virtual reality. Students will also communicate with teachers and students all over the world by video-conferencing. There are many advantages to this. For example, a class of British students learning French will have the chance to practise live with French students in a classroom in Paris.

2 Nanorobots

Nanorobots are tiny machines that can travel through our bodies and repair damage. Many scientists think that after 2020 they will probably be common in everyday life. For example, when you have a stomachache you can swallow a strawberry-flavoured robot which will make a video of the problems in your stomach. Then your doctor will watch the video and decide what the problem is.

3 Medicine

New drugs like Prozac® are very successful at the moment. Some people think that in the next decade there may be new medicines which will stop violent or antisocial behaviour. Experts believe this will certainly be cheaper than keeping people in prison. But this is very controversial - many people think it is wrong to use medicines to control people's personalities and emotions.

4 New transport technology

Some people think that big family cars might disappear in the next thirty years. It is possible that cars will have space for only one or two people. Computers will drive the car for you - so, for example, you might 'drive' from Paris to London while you sleep! Petrol definitely won't be cheaper in the future so, more and more cars will probably use solar energy instead of petrol.

READING AND SPEAKING

1 In pairs, discuss what changes new technology will bring to people's lives. Use a dictionary if you need to. More than one answer is possible.

New technology:
- The Internet
- New drugs
- Tiny robots
- Solar energy
- Mobile phones

Changes to people's lives:
- will monitor our health.
- will replace petrol in cars.
- will make education more exciting.
- may help to reduce crime.
- will change the way we do our shopping.
- will replace personal diaries.

A I think the Internet will change the way we do our shopping.
B I think the Internet will make education more exciting.

2 Read the website quickly. Are any of the predictions in the text similar to yours?

3 **CD ROM** Read the website again. Tick true and cross false.

1 Paper will disappear from classrooms in the future. ☐
2 Students will fly to the Arctic for a day. ☐
3 The Internet will be useful for learning languages. ☐
4 It will be unusual to use nanorobots after 2020. ☐
5 Not everybody supports drugs which can stop violent behaviour. ☐
6 It is possible that cars will be smaller in the future. ☐
7 Petrol will become less popular as a fuel for cars. ☐

4 Work in pairs and answer the questions.

- Which of the ideas from the text do you find the most exciting? Why?
- Which ideas in the text do you find worrying? Why?

A I like the idea of talking to other students in a foreign language on the Internet. I think it's a very good way to learn.
B I don't like the idea of using drugs to control people's behaviour ...

5 Study Speak Out. Underline examples of each expression on the website.

SPEAK OUT | Talking about probability

VERY CERTAIN
Computers **will definitely/certainly be** cheaper.

QUITE CERTAIN
Mobile phones **will probably be** cheaper in the future.

POSSIBLE
Perhaps air travel **will be** cheaper in the future.
It is possible that air travel **will be** cheaper in the future.
Air travel **may/might be** cheaper in the future.

UNLIKELY
Cars **probably won't be** cheaper in the future.

VERY UNLIKELY
Petrol **definitely/certainly won't be** cheaper in the future.

---

6 **CD 2.14** Listen and complete the predictions. Then listen again and match predictions 1–4 with explanations a–d. Which prediction is most certain?

1 People will _____ stop wearing glasses in the future.
2 _____ people will be more interested in religion in 2025.
3 It will _____ be more common for retired people to study something new.
4 People will _____ travel more in the future.

a People will live longer and have more free time.
b Laser technology will be cheap.
c People will be bored with technology.
d Air travel will be cheaper.

Mind the trap!

When you make a negative prediction with *think*, use the negative form of *think* and not of *will*:

I **don't think** it **will** rain. NOT ~~I think it won't rain~~.

---

7 In pairs, decide if the predictions below will happen in your country in the next thirty years.

1 People will stop using their cars.
2 Record shops will disappear – everyone will buy their music on the Internet.
3 Most people will work from home.
4 People will watch TV on their mobile phones.

People definitely won't stop using their cars.

8 Work in groups. What are the chances that you will do these things before your thirtieth birthday?

- have children
- have a good job
- own a car
- get married
- start your own company

I think I'll definitely have children before I'm thirty.

Vote THE INDEPENDENT DEM ID CRATS

ID'S PROMISES TO YOU

- We all agree that public transport is a waste of public money. If we win, we will reduce the price of petrol. Travelling by car will be cheaper than ever before.

- EGO wants to close many universities and colleges. ID will spend more on education if we win on June 9. If we don't win, millions of young people won't have the chance to have a good, free university education.

- We will lower taxes for small businesses. If we win, we will help to create thousands of new jobs for young people.

- Our country needs cheaper electricity to help the economy. We will build more power stations if we win.

VOTE FOR US ON JUNE 9!
"Putting You First"

GRAMMAR AND WRITING

1. **Read the two election leaflets and answer the questions.**

   Which party wants to:
   1 spend less on education?
   2 make car travel more expensive?
   3 make electricity cheaper?
   4 improve public transport?

2. **Work in pairs. Would you vote for either of these political parties? Which ideas do you like/dislike?**

   A I think it's a good idea to increase/protect/improve/create ... .
   B I think it's wrong to help/lower/limit/spend more on ... .

Work it out

3. **Look at the sentence and answer the questions.**

   If we win, we will reduce the price of petrol.

   1 Is it possible or realistic that this situation will happen in the future?
   2 Which tense is used after *if*?
   3 Which tense is used in the other part of the sentence?

Check it out

First conditional
We use the first conditional to talk about a realistic situation that will/might happen in the future.

The condition   **The result**
If + Present Simple,   *will* + infinitive

If we **win**, we **will spend** more money on public transport.
If we **don't win**, millions of young people **won't have** the chance to have a good, free university education.

4. **Find other examples of the first conditional in the election leaflets.**

5. **Complete the sentences with the correct form of the verbs in brackets.**

   1 It _____ (be) cheaper to travel by car if we _____ (lower) the price of petrol.
   2 There _____ (be) more new jobs if we _____ (reduce) taxes for small businesses.
   3 If we _____ (spend) more on public transport, pollution in towns _____ (not be) so bad.
   4 Many animals and plants _____ (disappear) if we _____ (not protect) the environment.
   5 You _____ (find) more information on how to join our party if you _____ (visit) our website at www.ego.org.
   6 If the leader of ID _____ (lose) the election, he _____ (resign).

EGO'S KEY PLANS

Universities are an expensive luxury. We will limit the number of free places for students at universities if we win.

- - - - - - - -

Our environment is in danger. We promise to create more national parks to protect our country's wonderful wildlife. We will also increase the number of recycling schemes in our cities. If you vote for us, you will help to protect the environment for future generations.

- - - - - - - -

Air pollution in our cities is a major problem. If EGO wins, we will spend more money on public transport – the key to cleaner air. We will also increase taxes on car owners.

TOGETHER WE CAN CHANGE THE COUNTRY FOR THE BETTER!
ON JUNE 9

6 Complete the sentences. Then compare your answers with a partner.

1 I _____ if I pass all my exams this summer.
2 I won't speak English if _____ .
3 If I get some money for my birthday, I _____ .
4 I'll earn a lot of money if _____ .
5 I'll be really disappointed if I _____ .
6 If _____ , I'll be really pleased.

7 Work in pairs. Ask and answer about what you will do in these situations.

- there's nothing interesting on TV tonight
- you can't fall asleep tonight
- the weather's good at the weekend
- the weather's terrible at the weekend
- there's a big class test on Monday morning

A What will you do if there's nothing interesting on TV tonight.
B I will listen to my new CD or visit my friends.

8 Work in groups. Write an election leaflet for a student party in your school. Use the leaflets in Exercise 1 and the ideas below to help you.

• improve	the appearance of ...
	the snack bar
• get rid of	the cloakroom
	the rules about ...
• introduce	school uniforms
	punishments for ...
	a better choice of ...
	exams on ...
	new rules about ...
• change	the rules about ...
	the timetable
• spend money on	decorating the ...
	more computers
• reduce/increase	the number of tests/ students/teachers
• open	an Internet café
	a second-hand bookshop

If we win/don't win, we will/won't ... .
If you vote/don't vote for us, we will/won't ... .

9 Invent a name for your party and present your ideas to the class. Then vote for the party with the best ideas.

VOCABULARY

1 **CD 2.15** Match headlines 1–3 with ecological problems a–d. Use a dictionary if you need to. There is one extra problem. Then listen to the news reports and check your answers.

> **1**
>
> *Experts say world's climate is 1°C warmer than 150 years ago*

> **2**
>
> **Doctors warn that water is not safe to drink**

> **3**
>
> Pollution from UK factories is destroying Scandinavian forests

a acid rain ☐
b cutting down forests ☐
c pollution of rivers ☐
d the greenhouse effect ☐

2 Complete the texts with the correct words from the box.

pollution   destroys   lakes   the Earth
temperatures   atmosphere

Acid Rain
Acid rain first became a problem in the Industrial Revolution, but it is getting worse today. ¹ _____ from large cities, especially from power stations, enters the ² _____ and then falls as acid rain. It ³ _____ forests and can kill life in rivers and ⁴ _____ . We can see the effects of acid rain in eastern Canada, Scandinavia and central Europe.

The Greenhouse Effect
The Greenhouse Effect describes the situation when the air around ⁵ _____ gets warmer because of gases which trap heat. This is a problem because if ⁶ _____ rise by 1°C, the sea level will rise by over 25cm and many cities will be in danger.

3 Cross out the verb that does not collocate with the nouns. Use a dictionary to help you.

1 help
  protect
  destroy
  limit
  } the environment

2 reduce
  increase
  recycle
  limit
  } pollution

3 sort
  recycle
  reduce
  protect
  } domestic waste

4 protect
  sort
  help
  save
  } plants and animals

5 replant
  cut down
  recycle
  destroy
  } forests

4 In pairs, look at the photo and answer the questions. Use expressions from Exercise 3 to help you.

1 Where are the people? What are they doing? Why?
2 Which of these ways of helping the environment are common in your country?

bottle banks   recycling paper
sorting domestic waste   lead-free petrol
replanting forests

'The machine of flying fire will trouble ... the great chief.'

Nostradamus, *The Centuries* published 1568.

LISTENING

1 Work in pairs. You're going to hear the story of Nostradamus. Do you know anything about him? Answer the questions.

- In what century did Nostradamus live?
- What is he famous for?

2 Read the gapped text and decide what kind of information you need to listen for to complete each gap (1–7).

A date/year ☐ ☐
A number ☐ ☐ ☐
A noun ☐
An adjective ☐

The Life of Nostradamus

His real name was Michel de Nostredame. Nostradamus was born in ¹ _____ in southern France. He had ² _____ brothers. As a boy he was interested in Maths and Astrology, but finally decided to study ³ _____ at Montpellier University. He completed his studies in ⁴ _____ and married a woman from a ⁵ _____ family. They had ⁶ _____ children. He started making his famous predictions when he was ⁷ _____ years old.

3 **CD 2.16** Listen to Part 1 of the recording and complete the text in Exercise 2. Don't worry if you don't complete all the gaps at once.

4 **CD 2.16** Did you complete all the information? Circle any empty gaps and listen again to complete the missing information.

5 In pairs, put the advice in Train Your Brain in the correct order. Look at Exercises 2–4 to help you.

TRAIN YOUR BRAIN | Listening skills

Finding specific information

a Mark or underline any gaps that you didn't hear the first time. Then listen again. ☐
b Look at the gaps in the table or text and decide what kind of information is missing – dates, names, places, numbers. ☐
c Listen and try and complete the missing information. Don't panic if you don't hear everything the first time. ☐

6 **CD 2.17** Use Train Your Brain before you listen to Part 2. Then listen and check.

The Books of Nostradamus

To begin with, Nostradamus started making predictions about the next ¹ _____ months. He published his first almanac in ² _____ . These almanacs were very ³ _____ , so Nostradamus decided to make predictions for several centuries into the future. He wrote in several different languages, French, Latin, Greek and ⁴ _____ . He needed ⁵ _____ years to finish his work. Nostradamus died in ⁶ _____ and the finished book was published ⁷ _____ years after his death.

7 **CD 2.18** Listen to Part 3. Choose the sentence which best summarises Mary's views.

a Nostradamus was wrong because he only wrote negative predictions.
b The predictions are interesting but I don't really believe in them.
c Nostradamus correctly predicted events that really happened, such as wars and revolutions.

8 Work in pairs. Student A, look at page 141. Student B look at page 142.

9 Work in groups. Make five predictions about your town/school/country for the next ten years. Show them to another group and discuss your predictions.

The world of work

Read, listen and talk about jobs and work.
Practise verb patterns.
Focus on reading for specific information; taking and leaving messages.
Write an application form.

GRAMMAR AND READING

1 Work in pairs. Do you know these jobs? Use your dictionary to check the meaning of any new words.

1 librarian, therapist, priest, accountant, scientist, nurse
2 engineer, computer programmer, pilot, police officer, doctor, architect
3 psychologist, writer, translator, fashion designer, teacher, musician
4 insurance agent, lawyer, judge, salesperson, businessman/woman, marketing manager
5 company director, banker, politician, TV presenter, reporter, actor

2 **Think Back!** In pairs, compare the jobs above. Which ones, in your opinion, are:

- the hardest/easiest?
- the most interesting?
- the most stressful?
- the best/worst paid?

A I think doctors have the most stressful job.
B No, it's more stressful to be a police officer.

3 **CD ROM** Do the personality test opposite and check your score on page 140. Do you agree with the results?

Work it out

4 Look at sentences 1–3. Match the form of the verb (a–c) that comes after the <u>underlined</u> verbs.

1 A teacher <u>should</u> be patient. ☐
2 She <u>decided</u> to become a vet. ☐
3 I <u>prefer</u> working on my own. ☐

a *to* + infinitive
b *-ing* form
c infinitive without *to*

5 Complete the table with the <u>underlined</u> verbs from the personality test.

Verb patterns

Verbs followed by *-ing* form:
prefer, miss, stop, practise, not mind, can't stand, _____ , _____ , _____ , _____ , _____ , _____

Verbs followed by *to* + infinitive:
agree, decide, learn, offer, promise, seem, wish, _____ , _____ , _____ , _____ ,

Verbs followed by infinitive without *to*:
could, might, should, _____ , _____

What is the best job for you? >>>

For each pair of sentences choose the one that best describes you.

1 A I <u>enjoy</u> studying for exams with a friend.
B I <u>like</u> learning for exams on my own.

2 A I'm good at remembering facts and information.
B I'm good at remembering jokes and funny stories.

3 A I always <u>hope</u> to get top marks at school.
B I <u>love</u> helping friends with their problems.

4 A If I don't like something, I'm not afraid of saying so.
B If I don't like something, I always <u>manage</u> to be diplomatic.

68

6 [CD 2.19] **Complete the sentences with the correct form of the verbs in brackets. Then listen and check.**

❝I can't ¹_____ (believe) it! I passed all my exams! I really don't know how I managed ²_____ (pass) Maths. Now I need ³_____ (decide) what to study at university, but the problem is that I don't know what I want ⁴_____ (do).

A few months ago I decided ⁵_____ (study) Biology, but now I'm not sure. It seems ⁶_____ (be) difficult to find a job as a biologist. I suppose I could ⁷_____ (become) a doctor, but it must ⁸_____ (be) a very stressful job. My mum says you can learn ⁹_____ (enjoy) anything, but I wouldn't like ¹⁰_____ (work) in a hospital.

I enjoy ¹¹_____ (work) with people. I don't like ¹²_____ (do) the same thing every day. I don't mind ¹³_____ (get) up early. I love ¹⁴_____ (travel) and I prefer ¹⁵_____ (work) outside. Oh, and I can't stand ¹⁶_____ (talk) on the phone for a long time. What's the best job for me?❞

7 **In pairs, discuss what is the best job for the girl is.**

8 [CD 2.20] **Listen to the three conversations and match the speakers with the jobs.**

artist   politician   musician   TV presenter
fire-fighter   police officer

1 Mr Jones   _____
2 John   _____
3 Marilyn   _____

9 [CD 2.20] **Complete the statements with the infinitive or *-ing* form of the verbs in brackets. Then listen again and match them with speakers a–c.**

1 I love _____ (write) songs.
2 I can't stand _____ (have) a routine.
3 I enjoy _____ (be) the centre of attention.
4 I don't mind _____ (wear) a uniform.
5 I hope _____ (get) the chance to play.
6 I'd like _____ (help) people.
7 I can _____ (do) things for people.

a Mr Jones ☐ ☐
b John ☐ ☐ ☐
c Marilyn ☐ ☐

10 **In pairs, write five true and five false sentences about yourself. Use verbs from Exercise 5. Read your sentences to your partner. Guess which ones are true.**

A I would like to be a musician.
B I think that's true./That's definitely false!

Try our personality test!

5
A I <u>must</u> finish my work before I think about going to a party.
B I <u>can</u> always find time to enjoy myself – even if I have a lot of things to do.

6
A I <u>want</u> to use my practical knowledge in my future career.
B I <u>would like</u> to use my imagination and my creativity in my future career.

7
A When I'm with my friends, I <u>hate</u> being the centre of attention.
B When I'm with my friends, I love being the leader.

8
A I <u>need</u> to have new experiences and meet new people very often – if I don't, I <u>start</u> feeling bored!
B I <u>avoid</u> being in new situations if possible.

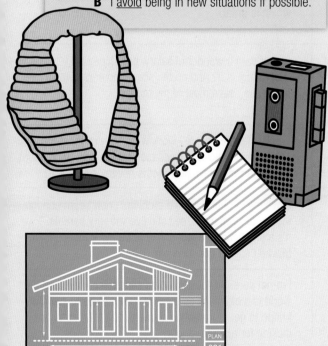

PLAN 021

Nice work if you can get it ...

Perspectives talks to two people with unusual jobs ...

Pete, 22

Elisa, 23

a ☐ I'm the resident DJ at *The Cube* – the best club in Wales. Come and see for yourself. We're open Fridays and Saturdays from 11p.m. till late.

I'm a fitness instructor on a cruise ship. We sail all round the world. This time last week we were in the Caribbean, and now we're off to Asia.

b ☐ I never really looked for a job as a DJ – it was just a hobby. I used to love hip-hop music, so I started DJ-ing at friends' parties. At one party there was a girl who was working at *The Cube*. They asked me to do an audition and that's how I got the job.

I used to have a part-time job teaching aerobics. But I always wanted to travel, so when I saw they were looking for someone to teach yoga and aerobics on a ship, I applied for the job and got it!

c ☐ I don't work every day, but when I work, I work hard. I play here two evenings a week and I do private parties too. My friends say I'm lucky because I don't work nine to five. But I do – the thing is I work from nine in the evening to five in the morning!

I work incredibly hard. Believe it or not, I sometimes work fourteen hours a day! But I can take a break occasionally, and I get a few days off for sightseeing, which is great.

d ☐ The money's not great – I make about 50 pounds a night and most of that goes on buying new music. But I can't complain. After all, I'm getting paid to do something I love.

I don't earn a wonderful salary, but money isn't everything, is it? And on the ship almost everything is free, so I save most of my money.

e ☐ The good thing is that I don't have a boss. Nobody can sack me if I turn up late!

I really like the people I work with. They're great fun. And I visit some amazing places too. But the best thing about my job is that I have six months holiday every year!

f ☐ The trouble with my job is that it's difficult to have a good social life. My girlfriend left me last year. She wanted to spend more time with me in the evenings, but I couldn't because of my job.

I love my job but there's a problem. I don't earn enough money to keep a flat, so I still live with my parents. It's a pity because I would like to be more independent. Maybe I should ask for a pay rise.

g ☐ No way. I love what I'm doing, but it's a job for young people. Anyway, I think it's good to change. You get bored if you do the same job for too long.

I'm not sure. Maybe. I'm doing something I love and the world is a big place so there is plenty more to see. But I hope to get a promotion soon. If I don't, I might start looking for a different job.

READING

1 Look at the photos of Pete and Elisa and answer the questions.

- What jobs do the two people have?
- Do you think they enjoy their jobs?

2 Read the text quickly. Which sentence best describes the general idea of the text?

1 Two young people explain how to find well-paid jobs.
2 Two young people describe their jobs.

3 Read the questions. <u>Underline</u> any key words which will help you find the answers.

1 Do you ever have any problems in your job?
2 Do you think you'll have the same job ten years from now?
3 How did you find such an unusual job?
4 How hard do you work?
5 What do you do?
6 What do you like about your job?
7 What's the money like?

4 Look at the words you underlined in Exercise 3. Use them to match questions 1–7 to sections a–g of the text.

5 Read before and after the key words and expressions in the text to answer the questions in Exercise 3.

6 Complete the sentences in Train Your Brain with the words and phrases below. Look at Exercises 2–5 to help you.

- underline
- the main idea
- similar ideas
- before and after

TRAIN YOUR BRAIN | Reading skills

Finding specific information

1 Read the text once quickly to get _____ of what it's about.
2 Read each question carefully and _____ the key words.
3 Look for the key words or _____ in the text.
4 Read _____ the key words to find the answer to the question.

---

7 📀 CD ROM Read the text again and use the advice in Train Your Brain to answer these questions.

1 Why do Pete's friends think he's lucky?
2 Why did his girlfriend leave him?
3 Why does he think he will leave his job eventually?
4 What did Elisa do before she started working on the ship?
5 What's the best thing about her job?
6 Why does she still live with her parents?

8 Use the advice in Train Your Brain and decide who the statements correspond to: Pete, Elisa or both?

1 _____'s job used to be a hobby.
2 _____ would like to earn more money.
3 _____ works for himself/herself.
4 _____ likes the people he/she works with.
5 _____ would like to have enough money to live on his/her own.
6 _____ is not sure if he/she wants to keep the same job in the future.

9 Find words and phrases 1–7 in the text and check the meaning. Then use them to complete sentences a–e.

1 a part-time job   5 turn up
2 a break   6 a pay rise
3 earn   7 a promotion
4 sack

a I don't _____ enough money. I'm going to ask my boss for _____ .
b You're working too hard. You should take _____ .
c Why don't you apply for _____ in the shopping centre?
d If you pay attention and work hard, you might get _____ soon.
e If you _____ late for work one more time, I'm going to have to _____ you.

10 Would you like to have a job with an unusual timetable? Why?/Why not? Discuss with a partner.

I wouldn't like a job with an unusual timetable because I don't like working in the evenings.

THE WORST THING ABOUT MY JOB IS THE STRESSFUL TIMETABLE.

HERBERT PERRIN
OFFICIAL PHOTOGRAPHER OF HALLEY'S COMET

VOCABULARY

1 In pairs, match jobs 1–7 with places a–g. Then discuss the questions.

1 checkout assistant ☐
2 fruit picker ☐
3 delivery driver ☐
4 guide ☐
5 receptionist ☐
6 secretary ☐
7 waiter/waitress ☐

a farm
b hotel
c office
d restaurant
e supermarket
f take-away pizza restaurant
g tourist attraction

- Which part-time or temporary jobs do young people often do in your country?
- Which jobs would/wouldn't you like to do? Why?/Why not?

I'd like to work as a fruit picker on a farm because I love working outside.

2 Read what the clown says and <u>underline</u> six more adjective + preposition phrases. What verb form do we use after prepositions?

'I'm <u>keen on</u> travelling. I'm interested in working with children, I get bored with being on my own. I'm quite fond of being the centre of attention. I'm really good at telling jokes, but I'm useless at telling people what to do. I'm not bad at falling down and oh, I don't mind getting wet!'

'I'm sorry Mr Bobo ... there are no vacancies for unemployed clowns right now.'

3 In pairs, discuss which of the jobs in Exercise 1 would be most suitable for the clown?

I think he should be a waiter because he's interested in working with people.

4 Work in groups. Use the adjective + preposition phrases from Exercise 2 to write seven sentences about yourself. Read your sentences to the rest of the group. Who is the most similar to you?

I'm very keen on working outside.

Mind the trap!

Job and *work* have different meanings:

Job (C) refers to specific activities and occupations.
As soon as I graduate, I'm going to start looking for a **job**.

Work (U) refers to something more general. It is usually uncountable.
I can't go out tonight. I've got too much **work** to do.

5 Complete these sentences with *work* or *job*.

1 Too much _____ and not enough fun can cause stress.
2 My ideal _____ is one where I could work outside with a group of friends.
3 Well done! You did a good _____ with my computer. It's really fast now.
4 Hard _____ never killed anybody.
5 If you're not busy right now, I have a _____ for you. Can you peel the potatoes?
6 I like _____ – it fascinates me, especially when other people are doing it!

Job Centre

SPEAKING AND LISTENING

1 Read the letter and answer the questions.

1 Who sent and received the letter?
2 Do you think Mr Baresi was happy to get it? Why?/Why not?

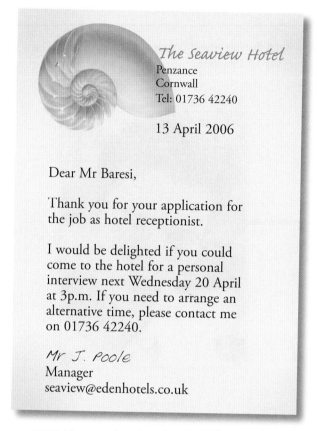

The Seaview Hotel
Penzance
Cornwall
Tel: 01736 42240

13 April 2006

Dear Mr Baresi,

Thank you for your application for the job as hotel receptionist.

I would be delighted if you could come to the hotel for a personal interview next Wednesday 20 April at 3p.m. If you need to arrange an alternative time, please contact me on 01736 42240.

Mr J. Poole
Manager
seaview@edenhotels.co.uk

2 (CD 2.21) Listen to Part 1 and answer the questions.

1 Who's making the call?
2 What's the problem?
3 What does Jeanine's flatmate offer to do?
4 What does Marco say he'll do?

3 (CD 2.22) Listen to Part 2 and answer the questions.

1 What does Marco ask Jeanine's flatmate to do?
2 What message does Marco leave?

4 Do you know how to say email addresses in English? Match symbols 1–5 with meanings a–e.

1 AAAA	☐	a	at
2 aaaa	☐	b	dot
3 @	☐	c	lower case
4 _	☐	d	upper case
5 .	☐	e	underscore

5 (CD 2.23) Listen to Part 3 and answer the questions.

1 Who answers the phone?
2 What's Jeanine's email address?
  a jeaninelebrun@MAIL_FREENET.com
  b jeaninelebrun@mail_freenet.com
  c jeanine_lebrun@mailfreenet.com

6 (CD 2.24) In pairs, study Speak Out. Put the dialogue (a–e) below in order. Then listen and check.

SPEAK OUT | Taking and leaving messages
A Hello?
B Hello. Can/Could I speak to (name), please?
A I'm sorry. He/She isn't here. Can I take a message?
B No, it's OK thanks. I'll call back later.	Yes, please. Can/Could you tell him/her that (name) phoned and (message) …
A OK. I'll tell him/her. Goodbye.

a OK, Mr Baresi. I'll let him know. Goodbye. ☐
b Hello, good morning. Could I speak to Mr Poole, please? ☐
c Yes, please. Can you tell him that Marco Baresi called. I'm afraid I'm going to be a little late. I won't be there until 3.30. ☐
d Seaview Hotel. Good morning. ☐
e I'm sorry, but Mr Poole isn't available today. Can I take a message? ☐

7 Which of these messages did the secretary leave for her boss?

Mr Poole
Mr Baresi called. He'll be here at 3 o'clock.
Jane

Mr Poole
Mr Baresi called. He's going to be 30 minutes late for the interview.
Jane

Mr Poole
Mr Baresi called. He wants to know what time the interview is.
Jane

8 In pairs, use Speak Out to roleplay the conversation. Student B, look at page 142.

Student A
You are looking for a summer job. Your friend, Jeanine, told you that her friend, Marco Baresi, has some information about a job in a hotel in England. Call Marco to find out about the job. If he's not there, leave a message for him.

• Say who you are and why you are calling.
• Ask him to get in touch with you.
• Spell your name and leave your phone number and email address.

WRITING

1 Read David's CV. Then tick true and cross false.

1 His birthday is in November. ☐
2 He isn't married. ☐
3 He doesn't go to school anymore. ☐
4 He has a full-time job. ☐
5 He can drive. ☐

2 Read the job advert below and David's CV. Can he apply for this job?

David Barnes

DATE OF BIRTH	8/11/1987
NATIONALITY	British
MARITAL STATUS	Single
ADDRESS	12 North Street, Southall, Middlesex, UB1 8BP
TELEPHONE	0208 599 6333
EMAIL	david_b@mail.uk

EDUCATION	1996–2005 Viliers High School
QUALIFICATIONS	• A-level exams: Maths, Chemistry
EMPLOYMENT	September 2005 – Present • Part-time Cashier: Texaco Filling Station, Ealing, London
OTHER SKILLS	• Driving Licence • Good knowledge of computers

WANTED

FULL-TIME DELIVERY DRIVER

For Southall firm
Must have clean driving licence

Excellent working conditions
Must be over 18 years old

Please phone **0181 874 5560** for an application form

3 Study **Train Your Brain**. In pairs, read David's application form below and compare it with his CV. Can you find any mistakes?

TRAIN YOUR BRAIN | Writing skills

Writing application forms

1 Type the form or write your answers in CAPITAL LETTERS.
2 Don't translate foreign addresses.
3 Answer all the questions.
4 If you don't need to write an answer, write *n/a* (not applicable).
5 Be careful with your spelling.
6 Always sign and date the form.
7 Give truthful information.

APPLICATION FORM

Scotpol Trading Ltd, Southall

POSITION APPLIED FOR
Title: DELIVARY DRIVER

PERSONAL INFORMATION
Surname: David   First Name: BARNES

Address for Correspondence: 11 North Street, Southall, Middlesex, UB1 8BP
Home Phone Number: 020 599   Email address: d_barnsey@clt.com

Age: ___ 16–18 ___ 18–21 ___ 21 or over

Date of birth: 11 NOVEMBER 1985

How did you hear about this job? ✗ Web Page ___ Newspaper

EDUCATION
Name of School:
Dates: 1996–2005
Exams taken: Maths, Chemisstry, Physics

OTHER SKILLS (including computing, driving licence, languages spoken) N/A

EMPLOYMENT HISTORY
Dates: From: 2003 To: NOW
Position: CASHIER

✗ Full-Time ___ Part-Time
Company Name/Address: Texaco Filling Station, Ealing, London

I certify that the above information is correct.

SIGNATURE: David Barnes   DATE: _____

---

4 Which of these things are suitable to put in the other skills section of an application form?

- clean driving licence ☐
- fluent spoken and written French ☐
- good at dancing ☐
- good team worker ☐
- swimming certificate ☐
- good knowledge of computers ☐
- non-smoker ☐
- qualified in first aid ☐

5 CD 2.25 Listen to the interview. Do you think David will get the job? Why?/Why not?

6 Read the job adverts below. Copy the application form in Exercise 3 and fill it in for the job you are interested in.

Jobsearch

Cawduff Castle
Needs assistant gardeners for the summer holidays

- No experience needed
- Friendly atmosphere
- Ideal for students
- Must be 16 or over

Talltown Turrets Theme Park
Requires cheerful and responsible young adults to work as welcome hosts

- The job involves welcoming guests to the park, operating the monorail system, parking cars and selling tickets.
- Hours: 5–10 hours per day

Bigbucks Coffee Shop
Needs serving staff in central London

- Some experience preferred
- Flexible working hours
- Must speak English and have an outgoing personality and good social skills

We are an equal opportunities employer.

7 Work in a group with students who applied for the same job as you. Read the application forms from a group who applied for a different job and check them. Choose the best candidate for the job.

VOCABULARY AND GRAMMAR

1 Complete the text with the correct form of the words in brackets.

NOT SURE WHAT TO DO AFTER SCHOOL? READ ON ...

What are you like?	You could be a/an ...
■ Good with language?	_journalist_ (journal) or _____ (translate)
■ An analytical mind?	_____ (law) or _____ (psychology)
■ The creative type?	_____ (art) or _____ (music)
■ Good with numbers?	_____ (account) or _____ (cash)
■ Good in front of cameras?	TV _____ (report) or _____ (act)
■ A practical mind?	_____ (engine) or _____ (science)
■ Want to help people?	_____ (politics) or _____ (therapy)

WANT TO KNOW MORE? COME TO THE CAREERS GUIDANCE MEETING – 3p.m.

2 Read the sentences and circle the correct words.

1 I don't feel well. I think I'm going to *faint / change / guess*.
2 If you turn up late again, you'll get *a pay rise / the sack / a promotion*.
3 The Greens want to *reduce / improve / increase* the number of recycling plants.
4 To *save / replant / recycle* our planet, we must cut pollution.
5 I *can't stand / don't mind / am keen on* my job. It's too stressful!
6 Politicians often make *fluent / controversial / violent* decisions.

3 Complete the second sentence so that it has a similar meaning to the first sentence. Use the word in bold and other words to complete each sentence.

1 I am sure that I will fail my exams. **pass**
  I _____ my exams.
2 I like swimming better than playing basketball. **prefer**
  I _____ playing basketball.
3 I will go for a walk if it is sunny. **rains**
  If _____ go for a walk.
4 It is quite likely that I will get the job. **probably**
  I _____ get the job.
5 Steve doesn't like working hard. **keen**
  Steve _____ working hard.

4 Complete the sentences. Use *will* or *going to* and the verbs in the box.

ask be crash fail find rise

1 Oh no! Look at that plane! It _____ !
2 The exam is really difficult. I'm sure I _____ it.
3 I believe scientists _____ a way to produce cheap and clean energy.
4 Experts say sea levels _____ by about 25 centimetres this century.
5 Don't worry. I really don't think you _____ unemployed for ever!
6 Sssh! This is a key moment in the film. He _____ her to marry him.

5 Complete the sentences with the correct form of the verbs in brackets.

1 If you _____ (do) that again, I _____ (tell) the others.
2 You _____ (get) wet if you _____ (not take) an umbrella.
3 If I _____ (get) the job, I _____ (tell) you at once.
4 You _____ (not get) a job if you _____ (not look) for one.
5 _____ (you call) me if the train _____ (be) late?
6 It _____ (not work) if you _____ (not switch) it on.

PRONUNCIATION

1 [CD 2.26] Listen and put the words in the box in the correct column. Then listen and check.

/dʒ/	/ʃ/	/tʃ/
danger	pollution	virtual

bridge   cheaper   elections   engineer
fashion   future   insurance   jeans
kitchen   social

LISTENING SKILLS

1 [CD 2.27] **Listen and circle the correct answers.**

1 Sonia Jefferson is a
  a guest at the meeting.
  b teacher.
  c student who is going to leave school.

2 Sonia thinks that being a tour guide is
  a always stressful.
  b sometimes boring.
  c very interesting, but sometimes difficult.

3 To become a tour guide you must
  a be an expert in history and geography.
  b learn some facts about the countries you are going to visit.
  c have a degree in tourism.

4 As a tour guide you also need to
  a be very fit.
  b speak two foreign languages fluently.
  c have a pilot's licence.

5 A good tour guide
  a is a good person.
  b knows how to talk to people.
  c laughs a lot.

6 Sonia recommends the job of tour guide for people who want to
  a have a routine at work.
  b earn a lot of money.
  c have fun and adventure.

READING SKILLS

1 **Read the text. Match headings a–g with paragraphs 1–6. There is one extra heading.**

  a Keep cool and win! ☐
  b Fly back to the future ☐
  c Mirror, mirror on the wall ☐
  d Read minds to detect crime ☐
  e Wearing your doctor ☐
  f What is *Nextfest*? ☐
  g Your friend the robot ☐

Want to see the future?

By Maggie Shiels

1 ___
Nextfest is an extraordinary exhibition where you can meet the most innovative minds and discover new technology from around the world and see the things that will change the way we live, work and play in the future. For example, …

2 ___
Brainball is a computer game with a difference: if you're too competitive, you lose. The more relaxed you are, the better you play. *Brainball* measures your alpha waves and the person who is the most relaxed can push the ball to the other side and win. I'm sure it will be a popular game with yoga experts and stressed parents everywhere.

SPEAKING SKILLS

1 **Discuss in groups. Do you think these things will happen in the future?**

1 You will win an Oscar one day.
2 Your country's football team will win the next World Cup.
3 You will get a part-time job in the next year.
4 A meteor will destroy the planet this year.
5 You will fall in love before Christmas.

2 **Roleplay this conversation.**

Student A
Your name is Thomas/Emily Richardson. You want to get a summer holiday job in the USA. Call Simon (a friend of yours who worked in the USA last year) to find out about the job. If he's not there, leave a message.
• Say who you are and why you are calling.
• Ask him to contact you.
• Leave your name, phone number and email address.
Your partner starts the conversation.

Student B
You share a flat with Simon Beaver. Someone calls him.
• Explain that Simon is not in, where he is, and when he will be back.
• Offer to take a message and write it down.
• Promise to give the message to Simon as soon as he gets home.
You start the conversation. When you finish, show your partner the message.

3 ___
The *Skycar* looks as if it belongs in a Hollywood film. It certainly lives up to its name: it can fly. It can climb at more than 2,000 metres a minute and reach speeds of 365mph. If you want one, it will cost you about $500,000! However, the head of NASA says that in 25 years 90 percent of people will be using *Skycars*. Just think of the accidents!

4 ___
If you're keen on fashion, *Nextfest* can show you the clothes of the future; fabrics which you can change by downloading styles from the web, clothes which look after your health and a biometric suit which monitors your body and gives you medicine when you need it.

5 ___
Another success is a humanoid robot which can walk, turn, climb up and down stairs – and even dance. *Asimo* mimics human movement and is friendly-looking. Its maker, Honda, believes it will be a big help to blind or elderly people and to those who can't get out of bed.

6 ___
Detectives will love brain fingerprinting. It is a technology which reads minds by measuring brain waves and your responses to words or images. It is the perfect way to decide who is a terrorist and who is not or who is responsible for a crime and who isn't.

If you want to see the future, come to *Nextfest*. It's open all this week at the State Science Exhibition Centre.

Love and trust

Read, listen and talk about love and relationships.
Practise the Present Perfect; phrasal verbs.
Focus on agreeing and disagreeing.
Write short messages.

GRAMMAR AND READING

1 Look at the photo. What do you think is happening?

2 **CD 2.28** Listen and read. Then decide who the people are.

1 Barbara ☐   **a** Ian's gran
2 Margaret ☐   **b** Ian's father
3 Monica ☐   **c** Ian's mother
4 Eddy ☐   **d** Ian's girlfriend

Part 1

Barbara	Ian, you haven't eaten very much. Is anything wrong?
Ian	I've got something to tell you. Monica and I have decided to get married.
Barbara	Oh, that's … nice!
Eddy	Have you decided on the date <u>yet</u>?
Ian	No, we haven't. But I've <u>already</u> bought a ring for her!
Margaret	That's great news! I'm so happy.
Ian	Thanks, Gran.

Part 2

Eddy	Ian has done a lot of stupid things in his life, but this is crazy! Monica hasn't finished college <u>yet</u>! Have you <u>ever</u> heard of such a thing?
Barbara	I've never been so shocked! They only met five months ago! How come he's got enough money for a ring? He's <u>just</u> started his first job.
Margaret	Excuse me, but haven't you forgotten something, you two? How old were you when you got married? Twenty – the same age as Ian. And you didn't have any money, did you?

3 In pairs, answer the questions.

1 Are Ian's parents happy that he has decided to get married?
2 Who seems to understand Ian the best?

Work it out

4 Read the sentences and tick the correct rules.

- Monica and I have decided to get married.
- Ian has done a lot of stupid things in his life.
- They met five months ago.

We use the Present Perfect to talk about:
- news and recent activities. ☐
- past actions if we say when they happened. ☐
- past actions if we don't say exactly when they happened. ☐

5 Look at how words a–d are used in the dialogue in Exercise 2 and match them with their uses 1–4.

a already ☐   c just ☐
b ever ☐   d yet ☐

1 in affirmative sentences to mean *very recently*
2 in affirmative sentences to say something happened earlier than expected
3 in negative sentences to say something has not happened (but it may soon), or in questions to ask if something has happened
4 in questions, it means *any time before now*

Check it out

Present Perfect

We use the Present Perfect to talk about:
- news and recent activities.
  We've decided to get married.
- finished actions in the past if we don't say exactly when they happened.
  Ian has done a lot of stupid things in his life.

Affirmative I/You/We/They have ('ve) gone.
He/She has ('s) gone.

Negative I/You/We/They have not (haven't) gone.
He/She has not (hasn't) gone.

Questions Have I/you/we/they gone?
Yes, I/you/we/they have.
No, I/you/we/they haven't.
Has he/she gone?
Yes, he/she has./No, he/she hasn't.

Time adverbials used with the Present Perfect:
Already and *just* in the affirmative; *ever* in questions; *yet* in the negative and in questions.

Mind the trap!

We do not use the Present Perfect with time expressions which refer to a finished period – *last week, a year ago.*

We met yesterday. NOT ~~We have met yesterday.~~

6 [CD 2.29] Listen and number the verbs in the order you hear them.

told   taken   gone   read   bought   decided
done   had   forgotten   met   eaten   been

7 [CD 2.30] Complete the dialogue with the correct form of the verbs in brackets. Use the Past Simple or the Present Perfect. Then listen and check.

A: ¹_____ you _____ (hear) the news? Ian and Monica ²_____ (decide) to get married.
B: No way! ³_____ he _____ (tell) his parents yet?
A: Yes, he ⁴_____ (tell) them last night.
B: When ⁵_____ they _____ (meet)?
A: They ⁶_____ (meet) at my party on New Year's Eve.
B: ⁷_____ she _____ (finish) college?
A: No, she ⁸_____ (not/finish) yet, but he ⁹_____ (already/find) a job. He ¹⁰_____ (start) work last month.

8 [CD 2.31] Complete the dialogue with the words below. Then listen and check.

already   ever   just (x 2)   yet (x 3)

Monica Well, have you told your parents ¹_____ ?
Ian Yes – I've ²_____ told them! Gran's really pleased but my parents aren't too happy.
Monica Oh dear. I'm so glad that my parents have ³_____ accepted the idea.
Ian I'd really like to see you. Have you finished your work ⁴_____ ?
Monica No, I haven't finished it ⁵_____ . Have you ⁶_____ felt that you just can't concentrate?
Ian Hold on a minute …
Margaret Sorry to interrupt. I've ⁷_____ talked to your mum and dad and everything's going to be OK.
Ian Thanks, Gran! Did you hear that?
Monica Yes, I did. Listen – I'll do my work tomorrow. We need to celebrate!

9 In pairs, use the ideas below to interview your partner.

Have you ever:
- meet/anyone famous?
- go/on a blind date?
- see/your favourite band in a concert?
- have/an argument with a friend/someone in your family?

A Have you ever met anyone famous?
B Yes, I have. I met … in a pub last week!
A I've never met anyone famous.

79

A LOVE THAT'S LASTED FOR FIFTY YEARS

Is there a key to true love? Norm and Jean Sell are about to celebrate their fiftieth wedding anniversary.

Max Murdoch asked them for their secret.

12 February 2006

Max: **So, how long have you known each other?**
Norm: We've known each other for almost 52 years.
Jean: Norm! We've known each other for more than 52 years. We met in 1953!
Max: **How long have you been married, then?**
Jean: We've been married since 14 February 1956. Valentine's Day.
Max: **Have you lived here since then?**
Jean: Not exactly. We've lived in Stretford since the wedding, but not in this house.
Norm: No, we've only been here for sixteen years.
Jean: Eighteen years, Norm. We've lived in this house for eighteen years. Since 1988.
Max: **How did you meet?**
Norm: Well, I used to be a policeman. I retired ten years ago … And Jean was the waitress in my local café.
Jean: It was love at first sight.
Max: **So, what's your secret for a successful relationship?**
Jean: I think you have to fall in love many times – always with the same person.
Max: **Have you ever fallen out?**
Norm: We've had a few little arguments, but we haven't had a serious argument for years.
Jean: No, not since Christmas Day 1977. Remember you …
Norm: We have a simple rule – if one of us is angry, we always try to sort it out before we say goodnight.
Max: **One last question – have you got any regrets?**
Norm: I'm just sorry I didn't marry Jean earlier.
Jean: And I've never regretted a single day.

GRAMMAR AND SPEAKING

1 In pairs, choose one of the photos and answer the questions. Use the ideas to help you.

  1 What can you say about the two people? Are they …?
    • in their teens/twenties/fifties/seventies
    • married/divorced/engaged/retired
  2 What kind of relationship do you think they have? How do you know?
    • romantic/caring/passionate/friendly
    • hold hands/kiss/be in love/hug

2 Read the text and see if your predictions in Exercise 1 were correct.

Work it out

3 Look at the article again and complete these sentences.

  1 Norm and Jean have been married for _____ years.
  2 They've been married since _____ .
  3 Norm was a policeman, but he retired _____ years ago.

4 Look at the sentences in Exercise 3 and circle the correct words in these rules.

  a We use the *Past Simple / Present Perfect* to talk about situations which began in the past and continue now.
  b We use *since / for* to say when the situation started.
  c We use *since / for* to say how long this situation has been true.

Check it out

Present Perfect

- We use the Present Perfect to talk about situations that began in the past and continue now.

- We often use *since* to say when the situation started or *for* to say how long this situation has been true.

We've lived here since 1956.
We've lived here for fifty years.

Mind the trap!

We don't use the Present Simple tense with *for* and *since* to talk about situations that began in the past and continue to the present.

I've lived here for four years. NOT I live here for 4 years.

5 Read the text again and answer the questions. Use the Present Perfect and the time expressions in the box.

Christmas 1977   1953   18 years   50 years

1 How long have Norm and Jean known each other?
2 How long have they lived in Stretford?
3 How long have they lived in their house?
4 Have they had a serious argument recently?

6 Read the sentences and answer the questions.

1 Ian has been my boyfriend for five months. Leo was my boyfriend for five years.
   – *Who is my boyfriend?*
2 Pat has lived here for ten days. Pam lived here for ten years. – *Who still lives here?*
3 Karen has been married for two years. Kevin was married for ten years.
   – *Who is still married?*

7 Decide if these expressions take *for* or *since*. Then choose four expressions and make sentences.

7 o'clock   10 minutes   Tuesday
a long time   ages   last night   a week
1 January   most of my life   2004

I haven't received a text message for ten minutes.

8 In pairs, answer the questions about yourself. Then interview your partner.

How long have you:
1 been a student at this school/college?
2 known your best friend?
3 lived in your house/flat?
4 liked your favourite band/artist?
5 had your pullover/this book …?

A How long have you been a student at this school?
B I've been here for three years.

VOCABULARY

1 Match the phrasal verbs in sentences 1–5 with definitions a–e. Use a dictionary if you need to.

1 He's <u>fallen out with</u> his girlfriend. They're not talking to each other anymore.
2 She's the most popular girl in the class. She <u>gets on with</u> everyone.
3 He's clever, good-looking and generous. I'd love to <u>go out with</u> him.
4 Oh no! My parents want me to <u>look after</u> my baby brother on Friday night.
5 I <u>split up with</u> Jim because we were always arguing.

a to take care of ☐
b to have a serious argument ☐
c to have a good relationship with someone ☐
d to end a romantic relationship with someone ☐
e to have a romantic relationship with someone ☐

2 Complete sentences a–c with the correct forms of the phrasal verbs in Exercise 1.

a I [1]_____ my girlfriend really well. It's the perfect relationship.

b Have you heard? Nicole [2]_____ Tom. He's depressed because she's the best girl he's ever [3]_____.

c I [4]_____ my mum again. We're not talking to each other! She wants to [5]_____ me all the time. It's ridiculous! I'm not a baby!

3 **CD 2.32** Listen to the speakers and circle the people they are speaking about.

Speaker 1   his *girlfriend / sister*
Speaker 2   her *sister / mother*
Speaker 3   his *girlfriend / mother*

4 In pairs, talk about one of your relationships. Use these expressions and the phrasal verbs from Exercise 1. Guess who your partner is talking about.

- She's very unfair/so easy to talk to/got a great sense of humour.
- She trusts me/gives me a lot of freedom/irritates me.
- We have a good relationship/a lot in common.
- We used to argue quite often.
- I used to get on with her really well.

A I get on really well with him.
B Is it your brother?
A No, it isn't … He gives me a lot of freedom …

81

READING

1 **[CD 2.33]** Complete the lyrics with the words below. Use a dictionary if you need to. Listen to the song and check.

alone   darkness   stay   too long   warm
wonder (v)

Bill Withers – *Ain't no sunshine (when she's gone)*

There ain't no sunshine when she's gone.
It's not [1]_____ when she's away.
There ain't no sunshine when she's gone,
And she's always gone [2]_____
Anytime she goes away.

I [3]_____ this time where she's gone.
I wonder if she's gone to [4]_____ .
There ain't no sunshine when she's gone,
And this house just ain't no home
Anytime she goes away.

And I know, I know, I know, I know …
I've got to leave the young thing [5]_____ .
There ain't no sunshine when she's gone.

There ain't no sunshine when she's gone.
Only [6]_____ every day.
There ain't no sunshine when she's gone,
And this house just ain't no home
Anytime she goes away.

---

2 Read the lyrics again and choose the best answers.

1 The singer and the woman are probably:
a good friends.
b husband and wife.
c father and daughter.

2 When she's not there, he feels:
a sad.   b happy.   c angry.

3 Does he know where the woman has gone?
a yes   b no   c he's not sure

4 Does he think she's going to come back?
a yes   b no   c he's not sure

5 Where do you think she might be?
a on holiday
b working in another country
c in prison

3 **[CD ROM]** Read the story opposite. Are these statements about the song, the story or both?

1 The woman has gone away.
2 The man is alone.
3 He knows he has to leave the woman alone.
4 He is sad without the woman.
5 He knows where the woman is.
6 He is afraid she may never come back.

4 Read the text again. Tick true and cross false.

1 The man hasn't talked to his wife for a long time. ☐
2 He doesn't know what she is doing in Madrid. ☐
3 The children have forgotten about their mother. ☐
4 The man sends his children to work. ☐
5 At the end of the story, the woman comes home. ☐

5 In pairs, decide which of the people in the story said these statements.

1 Wake up! Mamá has come home.

2 I've just come from the airport.

3 We've missed you so much.

4 Have you brought me a present?

5 I haven't found a job yet. There's no work here.

6 I've earned enough money. We can move away from here.

7 I've taken them to school every day all the time you've been away.

8 I've been away for two years, but now I'm here to stay.

6 Match the underlined words (1–7) in the text with the people or places they refer to (a–g).

a the man ☐   e the man's wife ☐
b Verónica ☐   f the children ☐
c the family ☐ g in Lima ☐
d in Madrid ☐

7 Discuss in pairs. Do you know anyone who has gone to another country to find work?

sunshine

In a poor district near Lima a young man steps out of his home – a tiny house with a plastic roof. He looks up at the early morning sky. Another day with no sunshine. The weather has been terrible recently. He can't remember the last time he saw the sun. Heavy grey clouds fill the sky and his heart feels cold with sadness. There's no sunshine when she's gone, he thinks. There's only darkness every day. And she hasn't called for so long. He wonders if she's gone for ever. He tries to imagine life without her. What if she stays over there in Madrid cleaning the houses of the rich?

[1] He turns as he hears a noise; one of the children is waking up. [2] They miss her so much. The house just isn't a home without her. Every day they ask him, 'When is Mamá coming home?' And what can he say? One day. Soon, my baby. 'And why isn't [3] she here, Papá?' Why? Because [4] they need the money, and there are no jobs, and [5] over there she can earn in a day what you earn [6] here in a month. It isn't easy to feed five hungry children. But it isn't easy for them to live without their mother either.

He sighs. Time to wake them up and get them ready for school. He knows many people who send their children to work, to wash cars or to beg, but she has always said that her children must get an education.

But it's hard. He misses her too. He misses her smile, her voice, the songs she sings even when things look black. And he knows she loves him. But why hasn't she called? Perhaps she's forgotten them. Perhaps she's decided to stay there. Perhaps she's found someone else. He feels like crying, but he can't. Not in front of the children.

A dog starts barking. He turns back to the house to start another day.

Suddenly, a ray of sunshine breaks through the clouds and lights up the doorway just as Verónica steps through the door. He feels the warm sun on his back. The little girl has just woken up and is rubbing sleep from her eyes. [7] She looks so like her mother. She yawns and he hears her mother's voice. He hears his name, 'Nacho! Nacho!' Is Verónica speaking? Behind him he hears footsteps. He turns round. The sun is too bright and he can't see clearly. He puts his hand up to his eyes, and then thinks, 'I haven't woken up! I'm still dreaming!' But then Verónica shouts out, 'Mamá!' And he knows that sometimes dreams come true.

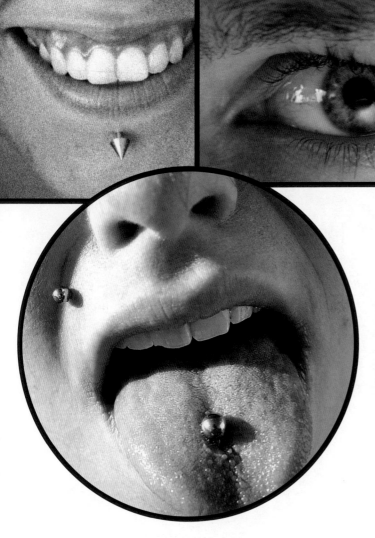

SPEAKING AND LISTENING

1 In pairs, look at the photos and answer the questions.

- What do the people in the photos have in common?
- Would you like to have a piercing?
- What do your parents think of piercings?

2 **CD 2.34** Listen and match people 1–3 with opinions a–c.

1 Anna ☐ **a** totally against piercing
2 Frank ☐ **b** tolerant of piercing
3 Jenny ☐ **c** in favour of piercing

3 **CD 2.35** Who says these sentences – Anna, Frank or Jenny? Listen and check. Then practise repeating the sentences.

1 <u>In my opinion</u>, a teacher should be a model for young people. ☐
2 Oh, come on. <u>You can't be serious!</u> ☐
3 <u>What do you think?</u> ☐
4 <u>If you ask me</u>, you have to be crazy to get a piercing. ☐
5 <u>That's right!</u> Piercings are horrible! ☐
6 <u>I see what you mean, but</u> it's Anna's body. ☐
7 <u>That's a very good point.</u> ☐

4 Complete Speak Out with the <u>underlined</u> expressions from Exercise 3.

SPEAK OUT	Expressing opinion	
Agreeing I totally agree. _____	**Asking for opinions** Do you agree? Don't you think …? _____
Disagreeing That's true, but … _____ I totally disagree. _____	**Expressing an opinion** Personally, I think … It seems to me … _____

5 **CD 2.36** Circle the correct phrase in the conversations. Listen and check your answers. Then act out the dialogues in pairs.

1 A Do you agree that teenagers watch too much TV?
 B *That's a very good point. / You can't be serious!* If you ask me, adults watch more TV than teenagers!

2 A Do you think that it's important for parents and children to talk to each other?
 B *I see what you mean / Do you agree?* – it's true talking can help your relationship, but it depends what you talk about.

3 A Don't you think that if you live in your parents' house, you have to do what your parents say?
 B I totally disagree. *Personally, I think / That's right but* my parents are my friends, not my bosses.

6 In groups, discuss one of the topics below. Use Speak Out and the dialogues in Exercise 5 to help you.

- It's important for parents and children to talk to each other.
- If you live in your parents' house, you have to do what they say.
- Good parents control when their teenage children go out and who they go out with.

LISTENING AND WRITING

1 [CD 2.37] In pairs, look at the photo below and answer the questions. Then listen and check.

- Where are the people?
- Do they know each other well?
- What do you think they are doing? Sharing secrets? Gossiping? Telling a joke?

2 [CD 2.37] Read the sentences. Listen again. Tick the true statements and correct the false ones.

1 Liz is wearing a blue top. ☐
2 Liz has just split up with Leo. ☐
3 Liz has got straight hair now. ☐
4 Sophie has seen Liz with a tall guy called John. ☐
5 Sophie thinks Liz has fallen in love with the tall guy. ☐
6 Hugh has decided to study Psychology. ☐

3 Find these abbreviations in the text messages below and decide what they mean. Circle the correct answer.

1 CU = see you / queue   3 w = what / with
2 @ = and / at   4 gr8 = great / green

1
I've split up with Sophie. She never listens to me. ☹ CU @ 8.
Options   Back

2
Liz has split up w John! I've just seen her new boyfriend. I wonder who he is.
Reply   More

3
gr8 news! I passed my interview! ☺ I'm in the café w your brother. Love you.
Reply   More

4 Read the messages from Exercise 3 again and decide who sent them.

Sophie ☐   Liz ☐   Hugh ☐

5 What do the abbreviations in the messages below mean? Then match replies A–C with messages 1–3 in Exercise 3.

1 U   under/you
2 n   and/no
3 mins   minutes/months
4 H & K hot and cold/hugs and kisses
5 IMO   in my opinion/I must object
6 2   to/toe
7 B   but/be
8 goss   gossip/goes

A
U must B joking. Phone me @ 9 n tell me all the goss!
Reply   More

B
Well done! ☺ I'll be there in 15 mins H & K
Options   Back

C
Don't panic mate! IMO u did the right thing 2 leave her. CU @ 8!
Reply   More

6 In groups of four, write a text message to each person in your group. Reply to the messages you are given. Use the abbreviations above to help you.

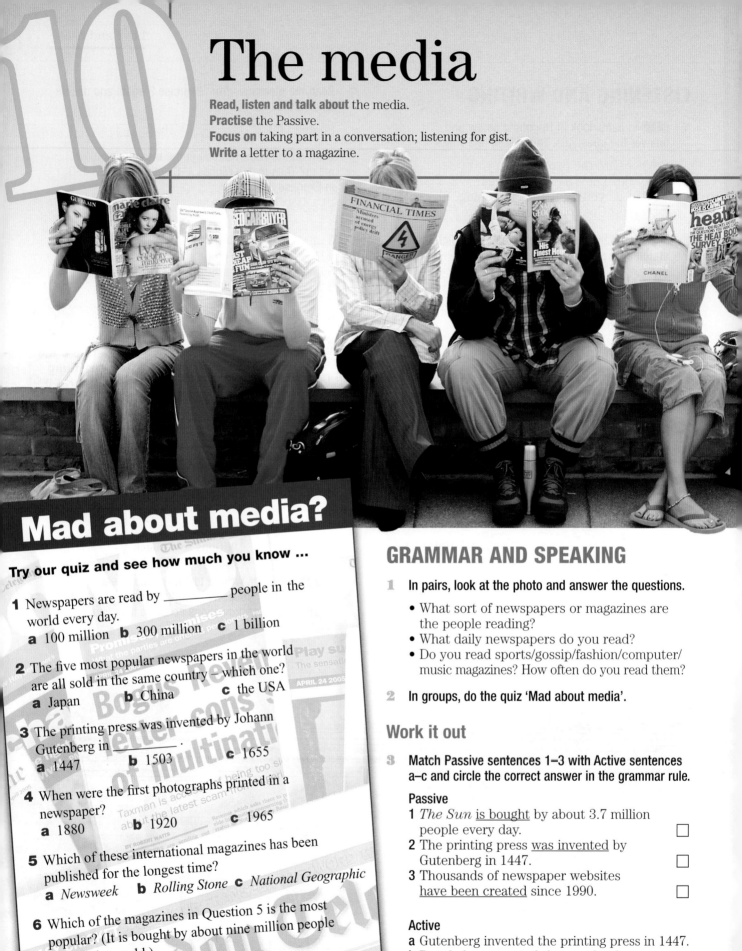

The media

Read, listen and talk about the media.
Practise the Passive.
Focus on taking part in a conversation; listening for gist.
Write a letter to a magazine.

Mad about media?

Try our quiz and see how much you know ...

1 Newspapers are read by _____ people in the world every day.
   a 100 million   **b** 300 million   **c** 1 billion

2 The five most popular newspapers in the world are all sold in the same country – which one?
   a Japan   **b** China   **c** the USA

3 The printing press was invented by Johann Gutenberg in _____ .
   a 1447   **b** 1503   **c** 1655

4 When were the first photographs printed in a newspaper?
   a 1880   **b** 1920   **c** 1965

5 Which of these international magazines has been published for the longest time?
   a *Newsweek*   **b** *Rolling Stone*   **c** *National Geographic*

6 Which of the magazines in Question 5 is the most popular? (It is bought by about nine million people around the world.)

7 *The Sun* is the UK's most popular daily newspaper. Every day it is bought by about _____ people.
   a 1.2 million   **b** 3.7 million   **c** 10.4 million

8 How many newspaper websites have been created since 1990?
   a dozens   **b** hundreds   **c** thousands

GRAMMAR AND SPEAKING

1 In pairs, look at the photo and answer the questions.
   - What sort of newspapers or magazines are the people reading?
   - What daily newspapers do you read?
   - Do you read sports/gossip/fashion/computer/music magazines? How often do you read them?

2 In groups, do the quiz 'Mad about media'.

Work it out

3 Match Passive sentences 1–3 with Active sentences a–c and circle the correct answer in the grammar rule.

Passive
1 *The Sun* is bought by about 3.7 million people every day.   ☐
2 The printing press was invented by Gutenberg in 1447.   ☐
3 Thousands of newspaper websites have been created since 1990.   ☐

Active
a Gutenberg invented the printing press in 1447.
b People have created thousands of newspaper websites since 1990.
c 3.7 million people buy *The Sun* every day.

   - We use the *Active / Passive* when we are more interested in the action than the person who does it.

4 Look at the <u>underlined</u> verbs in sentences 1–3 in Exercise 3 and complete the rules with the words in the box.

am/is/are   has been/have been   was/were

We form:
- the Present Simple Passive with _____ and the Past Participle.
- the Past Simple Passive with _____ and the Past Participle.
- the Present Perfect Passive with _____ and the Past Participle.

Check it out

The Passive

We use the Passive when we are more interested in the action than the person who does it. We often use the word *by* to indicate who does the action.

To form the Passive we use the correct form of the verb *to be* and the Past Participle.

The Sun is bought by about 3.7 million people every day. (Present Simple)
When was the printing press invented? (Past Simple)
This story has not been reported in the press. (Present Perfect)

5 Find more examples of the Passive in the quiz. What tense are they?

6 In pairs, complete extracts a–f with the correct passive form of the verbs in brackets. Then match them with the newspaper sections below.

gossip column ☐   readers' letters ☐
science ☐   TV guide ☐
international news ☐   sports ☐

a In your article you say that every year hundreds of cyclists ¹_____ (kill) by drivers. How many car drivers ²_____ (kill) by bicycles last year?

b The world 100 metres record ³_____ (break) for the second time this week!

c A new planet ⁴_____ (find) in the constellation Aquarius. The planet ⁵_____ (discover) by astronomers in California early last week.

d Jimmy Deep stars in this comedy. Deep ⁶_____ (not/ask) to play comic roles very often, but he is really funny.

e Glamour couple Chrissie Butros and Spike Dare ⁷_____ (photograph) everywhere they go. It's part of their daily life. But you've never seen photos like these ones!

f More than 2,500 people ⁸_____ (kill) in an earthquake in Iran. The earthquake measured 6.7 on the Richter scale.

7 In pairs, look at the words and phrases in Exercise 6 and answer the questions.

- Which section of a newspaper do you read first?
- Which sections do you never read? Why?

8 Complete each sentence using the Passive so that it means the same as the sentence above it.

1 In the early 1960s people proposed the idea of computer networks.
In the early 1960s the idea of computer networks was proposed .

2 In 1965 somebody connected two computers by telephone across the USA.
In 1965 two computers _____ .

3 Ray Tomlinson invented email in 1972.
Email _____ .

4 We don't know the exact number of websites.
The exact number of websites _____ .

5 Search engines have counted at least eight billion web pages.
At least eight billion web pages _____ .

6 Today over a billion people use the Internet.
Today the Internet _____ .

TV or not TV?

Anti-TV groups are organising another *TV Turnoff Week*.
Jacqui Carlton asks if TV really is such a bad thing.

A Every year, during the last week in April, people are invited to turn off their TVs for a week and to do something more useful. Since 1995, *TV Turnoff Week* has been organised by anti-TV campaigners in the USA and the UK. Organisers believe that 24 million people have given up television for a week and that afterwards 80 percent of them watched less TV and about 20 percent stopped watching television completely.

B But can't television be educational? Doesn't TV news tell us more about what is happening in the world than any other type of media? Anti-TV groups don't agree. 'Television is hopeless at explaining the reasons behind the news,' they argue. 'We often watch shocking TV pictures of wars, social problems or famine but we often don't understand why these problems started.' Campaigners also say that watching TV is a passive activity. The average person spends two months of the year in front of the television. This means that many people don't get enough exercise – or use their brains. There are other negative effects too – families spend less time talking to each other and TVs are often used as babysitters. Campaigners are also worried about the influence that TV has on children and young adults – for example, the average 19-year-old American has watched 350,000 commercials and 18,000 murders on television.

C So there are certainly convincing arguments to turn off the TV. But what do the anti-TV groups recommend instead of watching your favourite soap opera? 'Read the *TV Turnoff Week* leaflets and you will find lots of ideas: go to the library, learn a musical instrument, play with your pets or start a diary. Or you could learn about your family history, do some charity work, or go to a museum. Read a newspaper or listen to the radio.' So, there are plenty of things to do, but are they as much fun as watching TV?

D Annie Davidson, a lecturer in Media Studies from North London doesn't think that watching TV is a passive activity. 'On the contrary, it gives you something to talk about. For example, when we watch a soap opera, we form opinions about characters or stories. And if you don't watch it too much, TV isn't necessarily harmful for your health. Life is busier and more stressful than ever before. We need a simple way to relax in the evenings and television is perfect.' So will Annie Davidson take part in *TV Turnoff Week*? 'I'm certainly going to watch less. There's a great drama on the radio this evening.'

TV Turnoff Week begins on April 25.

Are you a TV addict?

1 When do you usually watch TV?

2 Do you ever watch TV in the morning?

3 How many hours of TV do you usually watch in a week?

4 Have you got a TV in your bedroom?

5 Do you ever argue at home about which programme to watch?

6 Would you like to live without TV for a week?

7 What do you enjoy doing instead of watching TV?

READING AND SPEAKING

1 In pairs, check the types of TV programmes below. Then think of a programme in your country for each type.

soap operas   documentaries   talk shows   comedy series
game shows   debates and discussions   reality shows
sports programmes   quizzes

2 Complete the sentences with the types of programmes in Exercise 1. Then compare your answers with your partner.

1 On TV in my country there are too many _____ and there aren't enough _____ .

2 The most popular programmes in my country are _____ , _____ and _____ .

3 My favourite TV programmes are _____ .

3 **CD ROM** Read the text and match headings 1–6 with paragraphs A–D. There are two headings that you don't need.

1 Turn off your TV ☐   **4** The positive side of TV ☐
2 Better things to do ☐   **5** Reasons why TV is harmful ☐
3 TV and education ☐   **6** Why TV is good for our brains ☐

4 Read the text again. Tick the true statements and correct the false ones.

1 *TV Turnoff Week* is a new idea. ☐
2 The organisers say that the week has been a success. ☐
3 TV news is the best media for helping us understand the problems in the world. ☐
4 The *TV Turnoff* leaflets don't suggest many different activities. ☐
5 *TV Turnoff* campaigners are against all forms of media. ☐
6 Annie Davidson believes that TV is good because it is a good subject for conversation. ☐
7 Ms Davidson is going to ignore *TV Turnoff Week*. ☐

5 In pairs, complete the table with arguments from the text. Can you add any more arguments?

The pros and cons of TV

Pros	Cons
• TV can be educational	• TV doesn't really explain the news
•	•
•	•
•	•

6 In pairs, find nine different alternatives to watching TV in the text. Can you think of any more ideas?

7 Complete the survey for yourself and two other people. Decide who is the biggest TV addict.

	Me	Daniel	Monika
1 When do you usually watch TV?	in the evening after my homework	only on Saturdays	in the morning at breakfast, in the evenings until midnight, at the weekends all day

SPEAKING

1 In pairs, look at the photo and answer the questions.

- What is the girl in this photo doing?
- Why do you think she is doing it?
- Do you think she is wasting her time? Why?/Why not?

2 [CD 3.1] Listen to the radio programme and circle the correct answers.

1 What kind of radio programme is this?
a a news programme
b a phone-in
c a debate

2 The caller is worried because her daughter:
a won't eat anymore.
b wants to leave home to study computing.
c is spending too much time on the Internet.

3 The caller doesn't know very much about:
a computers and the Internet.
b mobile phones.
c her daughter's school work.

3 [CD 3.1] Study Speak Out. Then listen again and tick the expressions you hear.

SPEAK OUT | Taking part in a conversation	
Asking for explanation • I'm not sure I understand. What do you mean? • What do you mean by *chat site*?	**Asking for repetition** • I'm sorry, I didn't catch what you said. Could you say it again, please? • Could you repeat that, please?
Hesitation • Well, you see, the thing is … • I'm not sure really … • Let me think … • How shall I put it?	**Politely interrupting** • That's very/really interesting, but … • That's true, but … • I'd just like to say … • Excuse me, can I just say …

4 [CD 3.2] Listen and choose the best replies.

1 a Could you repeat that, please?
b How shall I put it?
2 a Let me think …
b What do you mean by DDR memory?
3 a Can I just say something?
b I'm not sure really.
4 a Excuse me, I'd just like to say …
b Well, you see, the thing is …

5 [CD 3.3] In pairs, complete the dialogue with phrases from Speak Out. Then listen and compare.

A Newspapers could disappear because of the Internet and 24-hour news channels …
B (¹Interrupt) I don't like reading on a screen. And what about public transport?
A (²Ask for an explanation.)
B I mean, it's easy to read a paper on a bus, but the Internet isn't so practical, is it?
A (³Hesitate) computers are getting smaller and you can access the Internet with …
B (⁴Ask for repetition.)
A Yes, I said you can connect to the Internet with your mobile phone.
B (⁵Hesitate) OK. The *paper* versions of newspapers don't have much future, but did you know that seven million people read *The Guardian*'s website every day?

6 In pairs, read the dialogue from Exercise 5.

7 Work in groups of four. Read the statement and follow the instructions. Use Speak Out to help you.

'Chat sites are bad for young people.'

- Students A and B find five arguments *in favour of* the statement.
- Students C and D find five arguments *against* the statement.
- Get together in groups of four and discuss the statement.

LISTENING

1 In pairs, answer the questions.

- How often do you listen to the radio?
- What is your favourite radio station?
- Look at the types of radio programmes below. Which ones do you often/sometimes/never listen to?

the weather   the local news   phone-ins
discussions/debates   the travel news
the world news   radio dramas
the sports news   comedy programmes

2 **CD 3.4** Listen. What kind of radio programme is it? Don't worry if you don't understand everything.

3 Make a list of key words which helped you decide what kind of programme you listened to.

4 **CD 3.4** Listen again. What is the main idea of what the reporter says? Circle the correct answer.

1 City scored an excellent goal.
2 City didn't play well.
3 The referee was terrible.

5 Tick three key phrases which helped you understand the main idea in the recording.

1 a very poor second half for City ☐
2 they started well ☐
3 the referee gave United a penalty ☐
4 City were absolutely terrible ☐
5 the fans were not happy ☐

6 Read Train Your Brain. Look at Exercises 2–5 and circle the correct answers.

TRAIN YOUR BRAIN | Listening skills

Understanding the main ideas

1 It *is / isn't* important to understand the context.
2 *Try / Don't try* to understand everything.
3 Listen for *key phrases / every detail* to help you understand the main idea.

---

7 **CD 3.5** Listen. What type of radio report is it?

8 **CD 3.5** Listen again for the main idea of the report. Use Train Your Brain to help you.

---

1 Think Back! In pairs, add as many words as you can to each category. Then compare your answers with another pair.

- **Sections in a newspaper**
  sports, ...
- **Types of TV programmes**
  soap opera, ...
- **Types of radio programmes**
  phone-in, ...
- **The Internet**
  chat site, ...

2 In pairs, use the pronunciation table on page 144 to understand words 1–6. Then match them with their definitions a–f.

1 /'dɒkjəmentriː/ ☐   4 /'tʃæt saɪt/ ☐
2 /'njuːzaɪdʒənts/ ☐   5 /fə'tɒɡrəfə/ ☐
3 /'hedlaɪn/ ☐   6 /'dʒɜːnəlistz/ ☐

a a person who takes photos professionally
b an informative and educational programme
c the people who write the stories in newspapers
d a few words at the top of an article
e a place to exchange messages with friends
f a place where you can buy a paper

3 Check the meaning of the words below. Then use the words in the correct form to complete the sentences below.

channel   station   tabloid   search engine
download   broadcast (v)

1 In my opinion, the BBC _____ better programmes than the other TV _____ .
2 _____ are the best way to find what you want on the Internet. You can _____ the programs for free.
3 My favourite radio _____ has no speaking. It's 100 percent music.
4 *The Observer* is a quality weekly paper. *The Sun* is a _____ which comes out every day.

4 In pairs, answer the questions.

- What is your favourite magazine?
- How often do you read it?
- What do you particularly like about it?

A

Your shout!

Got an opinion?
Tell the editor! Judy Punch

**The big issue: Read this week's star
letter from Edward Thistlewaite**

Just what is wrong with today's young people?

Dear Editor,
I am writing in connection with Julie Boyle's article 'Just what is wrong with today's young people?' in last Saturday's newspaper. I must say I agree with many things that were mentioned by the author.

First of all, Ms Boyle believes that young people are lazy. I totally agree. I am shocked at the poor physical health of teenagers today. They say they can't exercise because they have to study. However, in my experience 'studying' is just an excuse to avoid doing anything.

Next, she says that teenagers are unpleasant. In my opinion, this is a very good point. What's more, when I go shopping, I am disgusted with the unhelpful service I receive from young people.

Finally, Ms Boyle says that young people spend all their time in front of TV or computer screens. This is absolutely true. Although there are many facilities in our town – the park, the library, the museum – they are rarely visited by teenagers. On the other hand, cyber cafés are full of young people wasting their time with computer games.
Yours faithfully,
Edward Thistlewhaite
London

◄ Back ► Forward ✕ Stop ↻ Refresh 🏠 Home │ AutoFill Print ✉ Mail

B

Address: @ www1.teenstuff.com/messageboards/shockhorror.htm

Teenstuff

Teenstuff > Message boards
How to send photos   **MP3s**   **Shock, horror! Old journalist attacks young people!**   **Downloads**

Originally posted by Surinder86

Hi everyone!

Did anyone see Julie Boyle's article on young people in last Saturday's *Herald*? Unbelievable! She seems to think that all teenagers get up late and then spend all day watching TV. But that's just not true. Most of the people I know who are my age spend their holidays travelling or working part-time.

She also says teenagers wear the same clothes day after day. No way! What planet is she living on? I've seen some statistics that show teenagers wash more often and take more care with their personal appearance than any other age group.

That woman doesn't think – she just repeats a lot of stereotypes and generalisations. And then she says that teenagers are unpleasant and never smile! I really think she needs to get out more. I mean, when I'm with my friends, we're always laughing and joking. I wonder if she has ever actually seen any young people!

Come on you guys, let me know what you think about this.

Love you all ☺ Surinder

Reply posted by Lisa

Favorites History Search Scrapbook Page Holder

WRITING

1 Read letters A and B and answer the questions.

   1 What is the subject of both letters?
   2 Which letter is more formal?
   3 Which letter was sent to:
     a an Internet message board?
     b a newspaper?

2 In pairs, look at the letters again and find the differences.

Which letter(s):	A	B
1 mentions the reasons for writing in paragraph 1?	☐	☐
2 uses phrases like *next* and *finally* to start each new paragraph?	☐	☐
3 mentions opinions from the original article?	☐	☐
4 uses the passive?	☐	☐
5 ends with *Yours faithfully* and full name?	☐	☐

3 In pairs, look at letter A again and answer the questions.

   1 Which things does the writer mention in the first paragraph?
     a the name of the article he wants to discuss and when it was printed ☐
     b some personal information about his hobbies and interests. ☐
     c He shows that he agrees (or disagrees) with the article. ☐

   2 What phrases does the writer use to show that he agrees or disagrees with the article?

4 Study Train Your Brain and check your answers to Exercises 2 and 3.

TRAIN YOUR BRAIN | Writing skills

A letter to a magazine

1 Use a formal style. Start with *Dear Editor/Sir/Madam* and end with *Yours faithfully* and your full name.
2 In the first paragraph mention the article or letter you are writing about and say clearly if you agree with it or not.
3 Start a new paragraph for each of your arguments. Use phrases like *first of all, then, next* and *finally*.
4 Quote opinions from the original article. Use these phrases to say whether you agree with them or not.
I totally (dis)agree with this.
I have to say, I (dis)agree with this.
In my opinion, this is very unfair/a good point/nonsense.

Mind the trap!

When we know the name of the person we are writing to, then we finish formal letters with *Yours sincerely* and NOT ~~*Yours faithfully*~~.

5 Complete Surinder's letter to the editor using letters A and B and Train Your Brain to help you.

> Dear Sir/Madam,
>
> I am writing in connection with Julie Boyle's article *'Just what is wrong with today's young people?'* which appeared in your newspaper last Saturday. I have to say I disagree with many things Ms Boyle wrote about.
>
> First of all, Ms Boyle believes that all teenagers get up late and then spend all day watching TV. However, in my opinion ¹…
>
> Next, the article suggests that teenagers don't wash or change their clothes. In my opinion this is ²…
>
> Finally, Ms Boyle suggests that teenagers are unpleasant and never smile. ³…
>
> I wonder what other readers think about this issue.
>
> Yours faithfully,
>
> Surinder Sodhi

6 Find these words and phrases in letter A, and then use them to complete the sentences below.

Although   However   On the other hand
What's more

   1 Some people say TV is too violent. _____ , it can also help us to relax.
   2 TV is fun and helps us to relax. _____ , programmes like soap operas can teach us to be tolerant.
   3 _____ it is true that some TV programmes are trivial, documentaries can teach us a lot about the world.
   4 Newspapers offer us old news. TV, _____ , tells us what is happening right now.

7 You have just read a newspaper article called *Why TV is bad for us.* Write a formal letter to the editor. Give your opinions on these points.

   • TV encourages us to be lazy.
   • It often gives us a trivial version of the news.
   • We don't use our brains when we watch TV.
   • TV teaches young people that violence is always the best answer.

VOCABULARY AND GRAMMAR

1 Complete the dialogue. For each gap write one word.

Kate Have you ever fallen in love with someone that your parents didn't get [1]_____ with?

Tina Yes, last year I had a terrible [2]_____ with them because of my boyfriend. I really fell [3]_____ with them! We even stopped talking! Fortunately, I [4]_____ up with him after a few weeks. We never really had a good [5]_____ , anyway. By the way, have you heard the news? Gary and Jill are getting [6]_____ . The wedding's next month.

Kate No way! I don't think it's going to work. They're too young.

Tina I agree. I think they'll be [7]_____ by Christmas.

2 Complete the email. For each gap write one word. The first letter of each word is given.

```
┌─────────────────────────────────────────────┐
│  ▣                   Dad!              ▣▣ ▣  │
├─────────────────────────────────────────────┤
│ Reply  Reply All  Forward  ▣ ▣ ✕ ⇧ ⇩  Follow Up  A ▾ │
├─────────────────────────────────────────────┤
│  From: julie@mailbox.uk                    ✉ │
│    To: sophie@mailbox.uk                     │
│ Subject: Dad!                                │
├─────────────────────────────────────────────┤
│                                            ▲ │
│ Hi Sophie,                                 ▓ │
│                                            ▓ │
│ I hope you're enjoying your trip. We're all  │
│ fine. Dad's retired now. I don't know if he's│
│ happy, though. He's become a news addict.    │
│ He gets up at 7a.m., goes to                 │
│ the ¹n_____ and buys two different        │
│ papers. I just read the ²h_____ , but he  │
│ reads everything. Even the ³g_____ column!│
│ He's even started talking about working      │
│ part-time as a ⁴j_____ ! And then he      │
│ spends the rest of the day watching TV!      │
│ Especially the 24-hour news ⁵c_____ ! He  │
│ never watches anything I like. No ⁶c_____ │
│ series, ⁷s_____ operas or                 │
│ ⁸g_____ shows. Nothing fun at all. If I   │
│ have to watch another nature ⁹d_____ ,    │
│ I'll go mad!                                 │
│                                            ▼ │
│ Love Julie                                   │
└─────────────────────────────────────────────┘
```

3 Complete the second sentence so that it has a similar meaning to the first sentence. Use the word in bold and other words to complete each sentence.

1 The last time I spoke to her was in 1998.
not
I have _____ 1998.

2 They print most newspapers in Nigeria in English. **are**
Most newspapers in Nigeria _____ _____ in English.

3 They went to that restaurant last month. **already**
They _____ to that restaurant.

4 Lucy is going to tell Mark tomorrow. **yet**
Lucy _____ .

4 Read the dialogue. For each gap circle the correct answer.

Dawn Hey, Karen! Congratulations! I hear you [1]_____ in love! Tell me all about it! How long have [2]_____ him? Where [3]_____ meet?

Karen We [4]_____ at a nightclub last Saturday, so we have been together [5]_____ almost a week now. I've [6]_____ met anyone so intelligent and handsome ... Anyway, what has changed in your life [7]_____ I last saw you?

Dawn Well ... I've [8]_____ started a new job. It's great. Have you [9]_____ had a job you really like?

1 a fall	**b** have fallen	**c** been fallen
2 a you know	**b** did know	**c** you known
3 a do you	**b** did you	**c** were you
4 a met	**b** have met	**c** were meeting
5 a for	**b** since	**c** from
6 a ever	**b** never	**c** yet
7 a for	**b** since	**c** ago
8 a yet	**b** since	**c** just
9 a just	**b** ever	**c** never

5 Complete the sentences so that they have the same meaning as the original sentences.

1 They got married in 1983 and they're still married today.
They've _____ .

2 We last went out together three months ago.
We haven't _____ .

3 They published the first edition of *The Guardian* in 1821.
The first edition of *The Guardian* _____ _____ .

4 About 400,000 people buy *The Guardian* every day.
The Guardian _____ .

5 Road accidents have killed more than 40,000 people in Europe this year.
More than 40,000 people _____ _____ .

6 We do not accept bad language on this message board.
Bad language _____ .

PRONUNCIATION

1 🔊 CD 3.6 Listen and put the words in the box in the correct columns. Then listen and check.

/aɪ/	/eɪ/	/ɔɪ/
bl<u>i</u>nd	b<u>a</u>by	n<u>oi</u>se

b<u>oy</u>friend   camp<u>ai</u>gn   c<u>y</u>clist   d<u>ai</u>ly
eng<u>a</u>ged   enj<u>oy</u>   g<u>a</u>me   headl<u>i</u>nes   p<u>oi</u>nt
s<u>i</u>te   sunsh<u>i</u>ne   v<u>oi</u>ce

READING SKILLS

1 Read the text. Match opinions 1–6 with people A–F.

1 It's a good idea to tell your parents about your new life. ☐

2 I love my parents but they don't give me enough freedom. ☐

3 Why don't you live away from home and become independent? ☐

4 I'm very sorry now that I didn't discuss things with my parents. ☐

5 I understand you. My parents don't listen to me either. ☐

6 People who complain about living at home don't know how lucky they are. ☐

☐☒

◀ Forward Stop Refresh Home AutoFill Print Mail

ⓐ http://www1.adviceforum.co.uk ▸ go

A *Posted by* **Amy** *at 01:24 on Feb 12th*

Hi guys! I need your advice. I'm a 19-year-old student in my first year at university. I love my new life, but I still live at home with my parents. I get on really well with them. They're really generous and they love me. The problem is that they treat me like a 12-year-old – I have to be home before 10p.m., they check to see if I'm studying and it's difficult for me to invite my new friends home. In fact, I've got a boyfriend now, but I haven't told them yet because I don't know how they'll react. Perhaps I should move out. What do you think?

B *Posted by* **Barbara** *at 01:45 on Feb 12th*

Personally, I really sympathise with what you are saying. I've had similar problems with my parents. I've tried to talk to them about it but they just won't listen!

C *Posted by* **Carl** *at 03:50 on Feb 12th*

I totally agree with your parents, Barbara. If you ask me, you are selfish! You probably have a more comfortable life than your friends who live away from home – and more money too!

D *Posted by* **Dennis** *at 06:19 on Feb 12th*

Carl, I see what you mean: there is a plus side to living at home that we often forget. The problem is simple. Amy's parents still think she's a little school kid, and they don't understand that her life has completely changed. But Amy, have you tried talking to them? Tell them about student life and how different it is from school. Then, perhaps they'll understand that you're an adult now.

E *Posted by* **Emilia** *at 08:39 on Feb 12th*

Very true, Dennis! Talk to your parents, Amy. When I was 19, I didn't talk to my parents and we had a terrible argument, and they threw me out, and I haven't seen them since then. I feel so bad about it now.

F *Posted by* **Franklin** *at 10:12 on Feb 12th*

I totally disagree with you Dennis. Amy, your parents just don't want you to grow up. The only solution is to leave home. Get a part-time job and rent a flat with your new friends!

SPEAKING SKILLS

1 Roleplay the conversation.

Student A
While you are studying in UK, you are taking part in a debate about television.
- Express your opinion that TV has a bad influence on young people.
- Disagree politely with your partner's opinion. In your opinion there is also too much violence on TV.
- Give an example of a programme which, in your opinion, has a lot of violence
You start the conversation.

Student B
While you are studying in UK, you are taking part in a debate about television.
- Listen to your partner's opinion and disagree politely. You believe that TV gives us a lot of useful information about the world.
- Ask him/her what kinds of programmes he/she thinks are violent.
- Agree with your partner but give your opinion of a programme you think is educational.
Your partner starts the conversation.

2 Describe the photo. Then answer the questions.

1 What do you think the relationship between the people in the photo is? Why?
2 Is it important to have a brother or a sister? Why?

Crime doesn't pay

Read, listen and talk about crime.
Practise the Past Perfect and articles.
Focus on dealing with new words in reading; expressing feelings.
Write an advert for a lost item.

CRIMINAL GAFFES

1

A gang of fourteen robbers broke into a bank in Naples and entered the basement. They were hoping to steal millions of dollars from the 8,000 safety deposit boxes there. But the men had an unpleasant surprise.

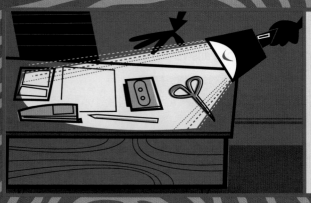

2

One night a Cardiff man was stealing equipment from the office where he worked. He didn't want the cameras to see him so he walked around in the dark. But he kept on walking into furniture and swearing. He took what he could and quietly left the building. Detectives arrested the surprised man the next morning.

3

A Detroit burglar arrived home after a 'successful' night. He was shocked when a few seconds later he opened the front door and saw his very happy dog ... and the police.

4

Neighbours in the city of Baku could hear music coming from an empty flat and decided to call the police. When the police arrived, the thief didn't even try to escape.

A

The man had left his dog outside the house he had burgled. When the police arrived, they shouted 'Home boy!' and the dog happily led the police officers straight to the burglar's house.

B

The guard with a key to the boxes had gone for a coffee and they couldn't find him. They hadn't prepared an alternative plan so they left with almost nothing.

C

After he had broken into the flat, the thief decided to make himself at home. First, he had a bath, and then he had something to eat and drink. After he had finished his dinner, he saw a piano in the corner and started playing it. He was still singing songs when the police arrived.

D

Had somebody seen him before he left the building? No, he had simply dropped an office dictaphone and it had switched itself on. Police later listened to the tape and recognised the man by his 'colourful' language.

GRAMMAR AND READING

1 Check the meaning of the words and phrases. Use a dictionary if you need to.

guard   robbery   thief   steal   arrest
escape   break into   burglar

2 Read stories 1–4 opposite. In pairs, guess why the crimes were not successful.

A *Perhaps there was nothing in the boxes.*
B *Maybe the guard saw the robbers and they ran away.*

3 Match explanations A–D opposite with stories 1–4. Were your guesses in Exercise 2 correct?

Work it out

4 Read the complete stories again and tick the situations that happened first.

1 a The robbers broke into the bank. ☐
   b The guard had gone for a coffee. ☐
2 a The office thief had dropped a dictaphone. ☐
   b He left the building. ☐

5 Study the sentences in Exercise 4 and circle the correct words and phrases in the rules below.

1 We use the Past Perfect to talk about an event that was completed *before* / *at the same time as* another event in the past.
2 With the Past Perfect we use *did + infinitive* / *had + Past Participle*.
3 The Past Perfect combines with the *Present Simple* / *Past Simple*.

Check it out

Past Perfect
We use the Past Perfect to talk about an action in the past that was completed before another action in the past. It combines with the Past Simple.
After he **had finished** his dinner, he started playing the piano.

Affirmative	I/You/He/She/We/They **had ('d) gone**.
Negative	I/You/He/She/We/They **had not (hadn't) gone**.
Questions	**Had** I/you/he/she/we/they **gone?** Yes, I/you/he/she/we/they **had**. No, I/you/we/they **hadn't**.

6 ▢**CD 3.7** Complete the story with the Past Perfect of the verbs in brackets. What had Pete forgotten to do? Listen and check.

Pete [1]_____ (spend) a month observing the Parker family, so he knew they went away at weekends. He arrived at their house early on Sunday morning. The alarm didn't ring when he broke the window because he [2]_____ (already/cut) the cable. After he [3]_____ (climb) through the window, he looked round the house. It was full of jewels and paintings. He [4]_____ (never/see) so many valuable things.

He smiled to himself as he drove away because he knew he [5]_____ (steal) a fortune. Suddenly he felt worried. [6]_____ (he/forget) something? Then he realised what it was. He hadn't ...

7 Look at the pictures of Kay's flat on page 141. Match verbs 1–5 with phrases a–e and say what the burglars had/hadn't done.

1 come in	☐	**a**	some pizza
2 break	☐	**b**	all her clothes on the floor
3 eat	☐	**c**	the money/the TV
4 throw	☐	**d**	the window
5 steal	☐	**e**	through the window

When Kay came home, she saw that someone had broken into her flat. The burglars had come in through the window. They had(n't) ...

8 Complete the sentences with *had*, *hadn't* or nothing.

1 Kay _____ felt angry because she _____ closed the window.
2 After the police examined the flat, they _____ found some fingerprints.
3 The police _____ found some fingerprints because the burglars _____ used gloves.
4 After the police _____ left, Kay _____ cleaned her flat.
5 The police _____ arrested the burglars two days later, after they _____ robbed another flat.
6 One of the burglars _____ explained that he had taken the hamster because he _____ always wanted to have a pet.
7 The burglars _____ left some of the pizza because they _____ already had dinner.

LISTENING

1 Check the meaning of the words.

dead   handgun   inherit   investigate
jealous   love affair   motive   murderer
personal assistant   silencer   suspect

2 [CD 3.8] Read the newspaper extract below. Listen to Detective Marlowe and answer the questions.

1 Where and when was Tina murdered?
2 Who called the police?
3 How was she killed?

3 [CD 3.9] Listen to Part 2 and match suspects 1–5 with motives a–e below.

4 [CD 3.10] Listen to Part 3 and match suspects 1–5 with actions a–e.

1 Bobbie ☐   4 Billy ☐
2 Nicola ☐   5 Christine ☐
3 Delia ☐

a left the party early
b was the first guest to go onto the terrace
c heard someone screaming
d had an argument with Tina
e was putting her coat on when someone started shouting

5 [CD 3.10] Match the beginnings and endings of the statements. Then listen to Part 3 again and check.

Bobbie   When we got there, Tina was dead … ☐
Nicola   It was the most horrible thing … ☐
Delia   I was working when … ☐
Billy   When I got nearer, … ☐
Christine I tried to help her, but … ☐

a she had already died.
b and Delia had already called the police.
c I had ever seen.
d I heard a shot.
e I saw she was dead.

6 [CD 3.11] In groups, decide who killed Tina. Listen to Part 4. What mistake had the murderer made?

TINA MURDERED

Teenage pop star Tina Squires has been murdered. It happened late last night during a dinner party. Tina, 23, was shot on the terrace of her luxury apartment near Central Park. The murderer had used a handgun with a silencer …

Bobbie Davies
Pop idol

Nicola Goodfellow
Actress, going out with Bobbie Davis

Delia Adams
Tina's personal assistant

Billy Squires
Tina's brother

Christine Cross
Tina's manager

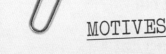
Tina Squires case

MOTIVES

a He will inherit Tina's money. ☐
b Tina had broken a promise to her. ☐
c She had stolen a lot of money from Tina. ☐
d He was angry with Tina because she kept calling him. ☐
e She was jealous of Tina and scared of losing her boyfriend. ☐

CONFIDENTIA

Romeo, Romeo, you're under arrest Romeo.

A twenty-one-year-old man appeared at Nottingham Crown Court yesterday, accused of vandalism. The man, Chris Austin, a graphic artist, admits committing the crime, but says he did it for love. The judge said that love was no excuse.

It all began in **1997** when **the Cooper family** moved in next door to the Austins in **Fairview Road**, Nottingham. The new neighbours had children of the same age, and at first they got on very well. They saw each other socially, they often **had lunch** together and the children, Chris and Jacky, used to walk to school together in **the morning**. Life was good.

A few years later, Chris and Jacky had fallen in love and were going out together. But then the two families fell out and the Coopers moved to a new house in **Ruddington** – miles away on the other side of town!

Love is strong, and the young couple continued seeing each other in secret. But then one day in **July** Mrs Cooper found out about the relationship and stopped Jacky from going out.

Chris was desperate without Jacky so he decided to prove how much he loved her.

The Cooper's garden is always full of roses at this time of year. But when the sun came up on **Saturday**, Chris had pulled up the roses in **the front garden** and used them to write the message, 'I love you' on the lawn. He had painted 'Chris loves Jacky' on the wall of the house. And he had poured pink paint over the Cooper's car.

Mr Cooper called the police immediately. **By John Deans**

GRAMMAR AND READING

1 In pairs discuss what you remember about Chris Austin in Unit 5. Then read the article.

Work it out

2 Look at the examples and complete the rules below with *a/an*, *the* or no article.

singular
A man appeared in court yesterday. The man admits committing the crime.

plural
They had children of the same age. The children walked to school together.

something unique
The judge said love was no excuse.

general statements
Life was good.

Articles
1 We use _____ to mention a person or a countable thing for the first time. (singular)
2 We use _____ to mention people or things for the first time. (plural)
3 We use _____ when it is obvious what we are talking about because:
• we have mentioned it before.
• it is something or someone unique.
4 We use _____ in general statements.

3 Read the text again and match the words in bold to each of the rules below.

a/an: names of job.   *a graphic artist*
the: family names, parts of days, rooms/places around the house.
Ø: days, months, years, street names, towns, meals.

4 Complete the gaps with *a/an*, *the* or no article.

It was early morning on [1]_____ Friday, the thirteenth of [2]_____ December, 1998. [3]_____ man walked into [4]_____ bank in [5]_____ Hastings Street, Vancouver. He was [6]_____ unemployed actor called Norbert Givens. He gave [7]_____ note to [8]_____ cashier. [9]_____ note said, 'Give me all your money. I have a gun'. [10]_____ cashier didn't understand, so he called [11]_____ bank manager, who told [12]_____ robber, 'I'm sorry. I don't speak English very well. This is a bank for [13]_____ French-speakers.' The robber took his note and went to have [14]_____ lunch. Later, he decided to try again in [15]_____ English-speaking bank. He showed [16]_____ same note and walked away with £500. So, it seems that sometimes [17]_____ crime does pay.

VICTOR LUSTIG

King con!

For Sale

A

Victor Lustig was one of the most imaginative criminals in history. He won and lost several fortunes, had forty-five false identities, and was arrested at least fifty times! Born near Prague in 1890, Victor grew up in a middle-class family and learned to speak five languages fluently. However, he soon turned to a life of crime and in the 1920s he emigrated to the USA.

B

In Missouri in 1922 he used his most famous <u>alias</u> – rich Austrian aristocrat 'Count' Victor Lustig. He paid a bank $22,000 for a very old farmhouse that nobody wanted to buy. At the same time he asked the bank manager to lend him $10,000. The man agreed and they exchanged envelopes. However, the envelope that Victor <u>handed over</u> did not contain any money, and Victor got away with both his original $22,000 and the bank's $10,000!

C

Three years later he returned to Europe. He had already made over $40,000 in the USA. One afternoon in a Paris café, Lustig saw a newspaper article which said that the Eiffel Tower was in poor condition. The repairs were going to be extremely expensive and a few politicians had suggested demolishing it! This gave Lustig an <u>ingenious</u> idea – to sell the Eiffel Tower.

D

First, he asked a <u>forger</u> to make some 'official' government notepaper. Then, as 'Deputy Director General of the Post Office' he wrote to five companies which he thought might be interested in buying the Eiffel Tower. He told the businessmen that the government had decided to demolish the tower and sell the metal from it. He explained that the Tower was already thirty-six years old and the architect had never planned to build a permanent structure. Because the government's decision was <u>controversial</u>, the businessmen promised to keep the plan secret.

E

The five company directors then made their offers to buy the Eiffel Tower. Lustig chose the highest offer, took the cash, and escaped to Austria to enjoy his money. Each day, Lustig checked the Paris newspapers for news of his amazing <u>con</u>. But there was nothing – the businessman, Monsieur Poisson, was too embarrassed to tell anyone how Lustig had cheated him.

F

So Lustig returned to Paris, wrote to another five companies … and sold the Eiffel Tower for a second time! However, this time his victim went to the police and Lustig had to <u>flee</u> to the USA.

READING AND VOCABULARY

1 Read the article. Match paragraphs A–F with the correct heading. There are two extra headings.

1 A money machine ☐
2 A plan in Paris ☐
3 Caught at last ☐
4 Explaining the details ☐
5 He does it again ☐
6 Take the money and run ☐
7 The 'Count' and the bank manager ☐
8 The origins of a thief ☐

2 Look at the <u>underlined</u> words in the text. Decide what part of speech they are and complete the table.

Nouns	Adjectives	Verbs
alias		

3 Read the text before and after the <u>underlined</u> words. Use the context to work out their meanings. Complete these definitions.

1 An _____ is a false identity.
2 A _____ is when someone believes a criminal's lies and gives him money.
3 A person who makes realistic copies of money, documents, etc is a _____ .
4 When something causes arguments, we say it is _____ .
5 When a plan is brilliant and original, we say it is _____ .
6 To _____ is to escape quickly, especially when you are in danger.
7 To _____ something is to give it to another person.

4 Complete the sentences in Train Your Brain with the words and phrases below. Look at Exercises 1–3 to help you.

- context
- main ideas
- part of speech

TRAIN YOUR BRAIN | Reading skills

Dealing with new words

When you come across new words in a text:
1 Don't panic – often you don't need them to understand the _____ of the text.
2 Decide what _____ they are.
3 Guess their meaning by looking carefully at the _____ .

5 Read the end of Lustig's story and match the paragraphs with the two headings you didn't use in Exercise 1.

G
Back in the States, Lustig continued to <u>swindle</u> people out of their money. One of his most successful ideas was a magic 'box' which could make banknotes. Of course, the box didn't work at all, but when he was arrested in Oklahoma, Lustig offered his 'invention' to a local sheriff. The sheriff accepted the <u>deal</u> and Lustig walked free.

H
But finally, in 1935, he was arrested for the last time. At the end of his <u>trial</u> the judge found Lustig <u>guilty</u> and he was sent to Alcatraz prison, where he spent the next twenty years. Victor Lustig, the king of cons, died in 1947.

6 Use Train Your Brain to work out the meaning of the <u>underlined</u> words above. Check your answers in a dictionary.

7 **CD ROM** Read the whole text about Victor Lustig again and circle the correct answers.

1 People still talk about Victor today because
a the police never caught him.
b he demolished the Eiffel Tower.
c he committed some fascinating crimes.

2 Victor thought of his plan to sell the Eiffel Tower
a while he was reading a newspaper in Paris.
b while he was still in the USA.
c when he was in prison.

3 The French businessmen thought Victor worked
a as a journalist.
b for the French Post Office.
c as a government minister.

4 Victor's victim, Poisson, didn't go to the police because
a he didn't want anyone to know how stupid he had been.
b he believed Victor had really sold him the Eiffel Tower.
c he admired Victor.

5 Victor sold the Eiffel Tower a second time because
a the first time his victim didn't pay him.
b it wasn't illegal.
c it had worked perfectly the first time.

6 Victor's magic box
a was a successful invention.
b was a con.
c only worked sometimes.

Telephone

VOCABULARY

1 Match the pictures 1–3 with the words below. Are these crimes common in your country?

a shoplifting ☐
b vandalism ☐
c mugging ☐

2 [CD 3.12] Complete the table. Use a dictionary if you need to. Listen and check.

Crime	Criminal	Action
1 _____	a vandal	vandalise
2 _____	a mugger	mug/rob/steal
3 _____	a shoplifter	shoplift/rob/steal
theft	4 _____	rob/steal
robbery	5 _____	rob/steal
burglary	burglar	6 _____
murder	murderer	7 _____

Mind the trap!

We use the verbs *rob* and *steal* in a different way.

A criminal robs a person or a place.
The gang **robbed** three banks in one week.

A criminal steals something from a person or a place.
They **stole** more than $1 million.

3 Who does it? Match the people with the actions.

a criminal ☐ ☐
a police officer ☐ ☐
a judge ☐ ☐

1 arrests somebody for a crime
2 finds somebody guilty/innocent of a crime
3 commits a crime
4 accuses somebody of committing a crime
5 breaks the law
6 sentences somebody to twenty years in prison

4 Work in groups. Read the questionnaire below. Decide if each crime is not very serious (1) or very serious (5). Use the ideas below to discuss your answers.

It's/It's not (really) … annoying/common/ dangerous/serious/breaking the law/ committing a crime.
It's (totally) … dishonest/immoral/wrong/ unfair to other people.
Everybody does it.
It can lead to more serious crimes.
It causes a lot of damage.

It's criminal!?

	1	2	3	4	5
Cheating in an exam	☐	☐	☐	☐	☐
Fare dodging (travelling by public transport without a ticket)	☐	☐	☐	☐	☐
Shoplifting (stealing things from shops)	☐	☐	☐	☐	☐
Software piracy (illegal copying of music, films, programs)	☐	☐	☐	☐	☐
Speeding (driving too fast)	☐	☐	☐	☐	☐
Vandalism	☐	☐	☐	☐	☐

5 In pairs, look at the questionnaire again and answer the questions.

• What is the most serious crime? Why?
• What can society do to reduce the number of crimes like this?

SPEAKING AND WRITING

1 CD 3.13 Listen to the conversation and circle the best options to complete the advert.

> ## LOST
>
> SMALL, RED LEATHER **BAG / PURSE** PROBABLY LOST OUTSIDE **BELSIZE PARK / CAMDEN TOWN** TUBE STATION AT ABOUT **5.45 / 6.15** P.M. ON NOV 8. PLEASE PHONE 0608999999 AND ASK FOR **GRACE / SARA** IF YOU HAVE ANY INFORMATION.
>
> ## REWARD!

2 CD 3.13 Study Speak Out. Then listen again and tick the expressions you hear.

SPEAK OUT | Expressing feelings

Shock and surprise
No way!
I can't believe it!
Really? It can't be true!
I don't know what to say!
I'm (so) shocked!

Fear
I'm so worried!
I'm so scared!
I'm terrified!
I've never been so frightened in my life!

Asking for explanations
What's wrong?
What's the matter?
What's happened?

Telling someone not to worry
Don't be silly/scared!
Don't worry/panic!
Take it easy!

Giving reassurance
Cheer up!
It's not the end of the world.
Everything will be all right/OK.
(I'm sure) there's nothing to worry about!
There's probably a simple explanation.

---

3 CD 3.14 Listen to the conversations and complete them with expressions from Speak Out. Then listen again and practise in pairs.

1 **Boy** Oh no! Someone's stolen my motorbike!
  Girl [*express shock*] _____

2 **Teacher** Congratulations! You got the highest mark in the exam.
  Student [*express surprise*] _____

3 **Little girl** Dad, I'm scared. I think there's a ghost. I heard a noise.
  Father [*give reassurance*] _____

4 **Teacher** I'm afraid your son was cheating in the exam.
  Mother [*express shock*] _____

5 **Man** Uh oh! One of them has got a gun!
  Woman [*express fear*] _____
  Man [*tell her not to worry*] _____
  They haven't seen us!

6 **Girl** I don't believe it. My dad got stopped for speeding.
  Boy [*give reassurance*] _____

4 Work in pairs and roleplay the situation. Use Speak Out to help you. Student B look at page 142.

Student A
You're shocked. You have just got to school and you want to call your mother, but you can't find your mobile phone.
- Tell a friend that you're afraid that someone has stolen it.
- Tell your friend that you're sure you didn't leave your phone at home because you phoned your boyfriend/girlfriend on the way to school.
- You think your friend has made a good suggestion. Thank him/her.

5 Write an advert for a lost mobile phone. Use the advert in Exercise 1 to help you.
- Mention the make/model/colour.
- Specify when and where you probably lost it.
- Give details so people can contact you.
- Say if there is a reward for finding it.

"HAS ANYONE HANDED IN ANY MONEY?"

Entertain us!

Read, listen and talk about art and entertainment.
Practise reported speech.
Focus on making and responding to suggestions.
Write short messages/notes.

GRAMMAR AND VOCABULARY

1 [CD 3.15] Read and listen to the review. Does the critic have a good opinion of the film?

> ❝ MDM studios **spent** $50 million on *Batwoman 2* and they **are already filming** *Batwoman 3*. But no sensible person will want to watch this nonsense – the dialogue is terrible and Elvira Preston **doesn't know** how to act. Simply the worst film **I've seen** in years. ❞
> **Marcella Brown**

2 Look at the photo. Read the dialogue below. Do you think the couple will go to see *Batwoman 2*?

Girl Oh look! *Batwoman 2* is on tonight.
Boy Yes, there was a review in today's paper. The critic said that the studios had spent $50 million on it and they were already filming *Batwoman 3*. She also said it was the worst film she had seen in years and that Elvira didn't know how to act. In fact, she said no sensible person would want to see it.

3 [CD 3.16] Listen and check your prediction in Exercise 2.

Work it out

4 Is the boy in the photo giving his own opinion (Direct Speech) or repeating what someone else has said (Reported Speech)?

5 Find sentences in the dialogue which match the sentences in Direct Speech. Complete the sentences in the table.

Direct speech	Reported speech
Present Simple 'She doesn't know how to act.'	**Past Simple** She said (that) she ¹*didn't know how* to act.
Present Continuous 'They are already filming *Batwoman 3*.'	**Past Continuous** She said (that) they ² _____ .
Present Perfect 'It's the worst film I've seen in years!'	**Past Perfect** She said (that) it was the ³ _____ .
Past Simple 'They spent $50 million.'	**Past Perfect** She said (that) they ⁴ _____ .
will 'No sensible person will want to see it.'	*would* She said (that) no sensible person ⁵ _____ .

6 Read the reviews of *Batwoman 2* below. Then complete sentences 1–6 in Reported Speech.

1 David Leake from *The Sentinel* said that Hollywood was starting to run out of ideas.
2 *The Standard* said that the plot _____ full of surprises.
3 *Movie Weekly* said that kids of all ages _____ it.
4 *The Daily Post* said that Elvira Preston _____ so uncomfortable.
5 *The Evening News* said that the special effects _____ amazing.
6 Jean Crowe from *The Herald* said that she _____ after fifteen minutes.

hat the critics say about **Batwoman 2**

❶ 'Hollywood is starting to run out of ideas.' David Leake, The Sentinel

❷ 'The plot is full of surprises.' The Standard

❸ 'Kids of all ages will enjoy it!' Movie Weekly

❹ 'Elvira Preston has never looked so uncomfortable.' The Daily Post

❺ 'The special effects are amazing.' The Evening News

❻ 'I left after fifteen minutes.' Jean Crowe, The Herald

7 Mandy told a friend about *Batwoman 2*. Read how her friend reported the conversation. What did Mandy actually say?

'I was talking to Mandy the other day. She had just seen *Batwoman 2*. She told me that <u>it was great</u>. She told me <u>the special effects were amazing</u>. She said <u>it was the best film she had ever seen</u>, and that <u>she was going to tell Tom about it</u>. She told me <u>I would have to go and see it</u>.'

I've just seen Batwoman 2. It's great …

8 Look at Exercise 7. Which verb do we use before someone's name or a pronoun?

Mind the trap!

We often use *say* and *tell* in Reported Speech. We use *tell* before a person's name or a pronoun (*me, him, her*).

She **said** (that) the film was great. NOT ~~She said me the film was great.~~

She **told** Chloe/her (that) the film was great. NOT ~~She told that the film was great.~~

9 Read the poem. Cross out two of the <u>underlined</u> words. Practise reading the poem aloud.

I told <u>her</u> that I loved her.
I said <u>her</u> my love was true.
She told <u>me</u> she would see me
And said <u>me</u> she loved me too.

10 Report these quotes. Then tell your partner which quote you like the best.

1 'I have never enjoyed working on a film.' *Marlene Dietrich, actress.*
2 'In the future everyone will be famous for fifteen minutes.' *Andy Warhol, artist.*
3 'I think it's so sad that there are so many musicians who don't want to change the world.' *Moby, musician.*
4 'Nobody really sings in an opera – they just make loud noises.' *Amelita Galli-Curci, critic.*
5 'A critic is somebody who knows the way but can't drive.' *Kenneth Tynan, critic.*
6 'Television is chewing-gum for the eyes.' *Frank Lloyd Wright, architect.*

Marlene Dietrich said that she had never enjoyed working on a film.

VOCABULARY

1 Look at the photos. Tick the types of film you see.

1 a cartoon ☐   5 a crime film ☐
2 a (romantic) comedy ☐   6 a thriller ☐
3 a western ☐   7 a biopic ☐
4 a horror film ☐   8 a science fiction film ☐

2 In pairs, match titles a–h with the film types 1–8 in Exercise 1. Then tell your partner what types of films you prefer.

a *Broadway Murder Mystery* ☐
Inspector Clueless investigates the death of a theatre critic.

b *This town ain't big enough* ☐
A gang of cowboys make life difficult for the new sheriff.

c *Assassination Time* ☐
The FBI tries to stop an attack on the President.

d *Birdz* ☐
Baby Bird is lost. A crazy cat and a friendly dog help him to find his parents.

e *Love knows no age* ☐
Judy falls in love with her ex-boyfriend's dad.

f *The Revenge of Rameses* ☐
An Egyptian mummy terrifies staff in the History Museum.

g *Ludwig* ☐
The life and times of Beethoven.

h *Titan Terror* ☐
In the year 2059, astronauts discover a life form on one of Saturn's moons.

3 Tick the positive adjectives and cross the negative ones. Use a dictionary if you need to.

<u>attractive</u> ☐   predictable ☐   <u>forgettable</u> ☐
<u>imaginative</u> ☐   <u>interesting</u> ☐   amazing ☐
awful ☐   dull ☐   fascinating ☐   terrible ☐

4 Study Train Your Brain. Use a dictionary to find out what prefix we add to make the opposites of the <u>underlined</u> words in Exercise 3.

TRAIN YOUR BRAIN | Dictionary skills

A dictionary can show you what prefix to add to a word to make the **antonym** (a word with the opposite meaning).

Popular /ˈpɒpjələ(r)/ adj **1** liked by a lot of people. opposite *unpopular*

5 In pairs, use the words below and the adjectives from Exercises 3 and 4 to talk about films you have seen.

actors   characters   dialogues   film director   plot
soundtrack   special effects

A The special effects are amazing.
B Yeah, but the actors are terrible!

6 Answer the questions below to write a short description of a film you have seen.

• What type of film is it?
• Who starred in/directed the film?
• Did you enjoy it? Why?/Why not?
• What did you especially like/dislike about it?

PERIVALE ARTS FESTIVAL

EVENTS

FRIDAY 12ᵗʰ August

Techno Night
A Meeting of Styles with 4 DJs
Place: Rotters Nightclub
Starts: 10p.m.
Admission: £12

Concert of Cuban Music,
Performed by Los Mutantes
Place: Civic Centre
Starts: 8p.m.
Admission: £5

Exhibition of New York graffiti
Place: Asder Gallery
Open: All day to 8p.m.
Admission: free

Perivale Choir Goes Jazz
Jazz standards including
Gershwin, Cole Porter
Place: Forum Theatre
Starts: 8p.m.
Admission: £4

Buster Keaton night
An evening of classic
black-and-white silent
film comedies
Place: Forum Theatre
Starts: 7p.m.
Admission: free

Poetry reading
Gilberto Mourinho reads from
his new collection of poetry
Place: Wembley Road Library
Starts: 6.30p.m.
Admission: £3.50

SPEAKING AND LISTENING

1 Work in pairs. Read the leaflet. Which event do you think is the most interesting?

2 **CD 3.17** Read the information about Sol and Helen. Which *two* events will they decide to go to together? Listen and check.

Helen and Sol are both students and don't have much money. She studies literature and he studies art. They both love modern music and dancing, especially salsa. Sol also likes jazz, but Helen doesn't. They are not very keen on old movies.

3 **CD 3.17** Study Speak Out. Then listen again and tick the expressions you hear.

SPEAK OUT | Suggestions

Making suggestions	**Rejecting a suggestion**
Let's go to …	I'm sorry but …
Do you fancy going to …?	… it's not really my cup
How about meeting at …?	of tea.
	… I'm not mad about …
Accepting suggestions	… I'm not keen on the
(That's a) good idea.	idea …
(That) sounds good!	… I'd prefer not to.
Yes./Sure./Why not?	Why don't we go to
(That's) fine with me!	… instead?

4 In pairs, take turns to make and respond to suggestions.

1 A How about/go/cinema?
B ☹. Why don't/go/club?
A ☺.

A How about going to the cinema?
B I'm sorry but I'm not keen on the idea. Why don't we …?

2 A Fancy/watch a film on DVD tonight?
B ☺.

3 A Let's/watch/documentary/TV.
B ☹. Why don't/watch/a quiz show?
A ☺.

5 In groups of four, read the TV guide and decide what to watch.

- Student A, look at page 141. Student B, look at page 142. Student C, look at page 142. Student D, look at page 142.
- Use Speak Out to help you.
- Try to find a programme that everyone can watch!

TELEVISION TUESDAY

IBC1
19.00–19.30
Love and Trust. (soap opera)
Episode 1,389
Monica tells Ian she's leaving.

IBC2
19.00–19.30
Film Night with Marcella Brown.
Marcella looks at this week's new films.

IBC3
19.00–19.30
Celebrity Vets with Wayne Dylan.
This week pop star Cherie tries working as a vet at Cotswell Animal Hospital.

The Smile Channel
19.00–19.30
Yes, EU Commissioner. (comedy)
Sir David has problems with his Brussels translators.

The Disaster Channel
19.00–23.30
Seconds from Death.
More home videos of disasters and catastrophes sent in by viewers.

A How about watching *Love and Trust*?
B That's fine with me!
C I'm sorry but I'm not mad about soap operas. Why don't we …

READING AND SPEAKING

1 **In pairs, answer the questions.**

- Is graffiti common in your town or city? Where?
- What do you think of it? Is it beautiful or ugly?

2 **CD ROM** **Read texts A–C opposite. Then match the writers with points of view 1–3 below.**

A Sandra ☐   1 against graffiti
B Teresa ☐   2 for graffiti
C Mike ☐   3 on the fence (can see both sides of the argument)

3 **Work in groups and follow the instructions.**

Group A: Read text A, and circle the correct words in sentences 1–5.
Group B: Read text B, and circle the correct words in sentences 6–10.
Group C: Read text C, and circle the correct words in sentences 11–15.

Group A

1 The best graffiti is sometimes *better / worse* than 'official' art.
2 *Only a few / Many* graffiti artists produce beautiful works of art.
3 Most graffiti is *attractive / ugly*.
4 Graffiti allows young people to express *political opinions / their identity*.
5 Graffiti is alright in some places, but not on *buildings which are in use / old buildings*.

Group B

6 You can find graffiti *everywhere / in some places*.
7 Most people think graffiti is *beautiful / ugly*.
8 Graffiti is *important / illegal*.
9 People may commit other crimes because they *don't like / have seen* graffiti.
10 Some graffiti artists risk their *health / jobs* when they paint.

Group C

11 Graffiti is an art form which has existed for a *short / long* time.
12 Graffiti from the past can give us information about *ancient cultures / crime*.
13 Graffiti is *colourful and attractive / funny*.
14 Some graffiti is fantastic and you don't have to *go far / pay* to see it.
15 People will *never understand / understand one day* that graffiti is great art.

4 **Form new groups with one student from each group in Exercise 3. Tell each other the text you read.**

5 **Read the article again and circle the best answers.**

1 Sandra Jameson:
  a was impressed by the graffiti she saw.
  b saw the graffiti in an art gallery.
  c thinks there should be an exhibition of graffiti.

2 Sandra thinks that it is alright to paint graffiti on buildings where:
  a the graffiti artists live.
  b nobody lives.
  c people live.

3 Teresa Powell:
  a doesn't think graffiti artists would like graffiti in their own homes.
  b often paints 'Teresa is cool!' on walls.
  c sometimes paints graffiti in her living room.

4 The 'Broken Window Syndrome' means:
  a people only paint graffiti on buildings with broken windows.
  b that one crime can lead to another.
  c sociologists invite young people to commit crime.

5 Mike Lees thinks that graffiti such as 'Terry loves June' is:
  a limited.   b quite creative.   c imaginative.

6 Mike thinks Van Gogh's paintings:
  a are the work of a maniac.
  b were only popular with critics.
  c are more popular today than when he was alive.

6 **Find words and phrases in the text for these definitions.**

1 A building where people can see pieces of art. [text A]
2 An adjective to describe someone who is very good at something. [text A]
3 Impolite or offensive words. [text B]
4 To use an aerosol can to write on walls. [text B]
5 Describes art that is new and very different. [text C]
6 The best examples of a great artist's work. [text C]

7 **In groups, discuss if you think graffiti is art or vandalism.**

Is Graffiti Art?

Sandra Jameson, art critic of *The Times*

The other day I saw some graffiti on an old factory wall. It was absolutely fantastic: imaginative and beautifully done. Much better, in fact, than a lot of art that you can see in art galleries and exhibitions. Unfortunately, not all graffiti is so beautiful. Although it is true that some talented artists started their careers by painting on walls, most graffiti has no artistic merit at all. It's just people shouting to the world, 'I exist!' I understand why they do it. Young people don't own any buildings, and spraying walls is a way of 'owning' a piece of where you live. But it's a pity it's often so ugly. I think we should tolerate graffiti on old abandoned buildings. After all, they can't look any worse than they do. But it's wrong to paint graffiti on the walls of buildings where people live or work.

Teresa Powell, Member of Parliament for East Swindon

Everywhere you go, you see walls covered in stupid names and swear words. I don't know anyone who thinks it is attractive. More importantly, graffiti is a crime. Where do these so-called graffiti artists paint? On private property. And that means they're breaking the law. I'm sure they wouldn't like it if I spray painted 'Teresa is cool!' on their living room walls. So why do they think it's alright for them to paint anywhere they want to? Sociologists talk about the 'Broken Window Syndrome'. When a building is covered in ugly graffiti, it's an invitation for young people to vandalise it even more. So graffiti encourages more crime. And finally, it's dangerous – many artists climb high walls or buildings or vandalise trains at night. When they have an accident, we all have to pay their hospital costs. Graffiti is not acceptable and it should be stopped.

Mike Lees, graffiti artist

A politician recently said that graffiti artists were vandals and that graffiti was a crime. I totally disagree. Graffiti is an art form. It's been with us for thousands of years. Graffiti has been discovered in the ruins of Pompeii, and it tells us more about ordinary life than statues and monuments do. And today graffiti gives colour to our grey city centres. It is true that some graffiti is limited – 'Terry loves June' is not exactly creative. But a lot of graffiti is brilliant and imaginative. It's radical, it's fun, it's beautiful … and it's free. Many artists in history have been misunderstood. When Vincent Van Gogh was alive, nobody wanted to buy his paintings, and critics said he was a maniac. Today, his masterpieces are sold for millions. One day people will understand that some of the greatest art of our time isn't in galleries, but on factory walls and urban trains.

WRITING

1 Read the email. Where is Pete inviting Rachel on Saturday? Who else is he inviting?

> **Saturday night!**
>
> Reply · Reply All · Forward · · · · Follow Up · ·
>
> **From:** Pete88@magic.com
> **To:** Rachel@mail2.uk
> **Subject:** Saturday night!
>
> Hi Rachel,
>
> I hope you're well. Guess what … I've just received four tickets for tomorrow evening!
> Do you fancy going?
>
> I've seen the rehearsals and I think it's going to be great (and I know you love Shakespeare, anyway). The play starts at 7.30 p.m., so let's meet in the café at seven. I'm inviting Mark and Vicky as well.
>
> I hope you can come – please phone if there's a problem.
>
> Best wishes,
>
> Pete

2 Read Pete's message to Vicky. Which words doesn't he use to make sentences 1–7 shorter?

1 I've got four free tickets for tomorrow evening.
2 Do you want to go?
3 The play starts at 7.30.
4 Why don't you meet me in the café at seven?
5 I'm inviting Rachel and Mark too.
6 I hope you can come.
7 Could you phone me if you can't make it?

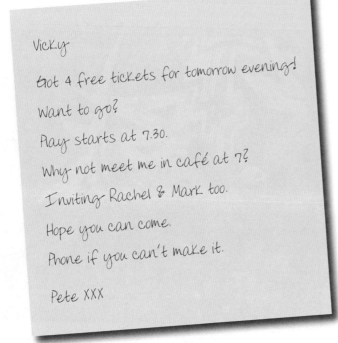

> Vicky
>
> Got 4 free tickets for tomorrow evening!
>
> Want to go?
>
> Play starts at 7.30.
>
> Why not meet me in café at 7?
>
> Inviting Rachel & Mark too.
>
> Hope you can come.
>
> Phone if you can't make it.
>
> Pete XXX

3 In pairs, compare the email and the note in Exercises 1 and 2. Tick things from the email which are not in the note.

1 The name of the person Pete is writing to.
2 Greetings and polite expressions – (Dear …, I hope you're well).
3 The time the play starts.
4 The place and the time to meet.
5 The fact that Pete has seen the rehearsals.
6 Pete's opinion about the play.
7 The other people he's inviting.

4 Look at Exercises 2 and 3 again and complete the guidelines in Train Your Brain with examples 1–4.

1 *do, have, …*
2 *I, you, my, …*
3 time/place of meeting …
4 *Dear …, How are you? Best wishes, …*

TRAIN YOUR BRAIN | Writing skills

Short notes/messages

1 In short messages we don't usually write:
- greetings and polite expressions like ᵃ_____ .
- unimportant information

2 We often leave out:
- pronouns like ᵇ_____ at the start of sentences.
  I̶ hope you can come.
- auxiliary verbs like ᶜ_____ at the start of sentences.
  D̶o̶ ̶y̶o̶u̶ fancy …?
- the definite article (*the*).
  T̶h̶e̶ play starts …

3 We often use the Imperative in short notes.
Phone if you can't come.

4 We must write the important details of the message like ᵈ_____ .

5 How many words can you remove from each sentence without changing the meaning? Check your answers on page 141.

1 I'll see you outside the theatre at 8 o'clock.
2 I'm going to the club tonight. Do you want to come?
3 Are you going home on Friday?
4 Do you fancy playing football tomorrow?
5 I'm arriving at the station at half six. Please wait for me under the clock.

6 In pairs, read the notes 1–4 and match them with places a–d where they were left.

a on a fridge in a typical kitchen ☐
b on a door in a student flat ☐
c on a desk in an office ☐
d on a computer screen ☐

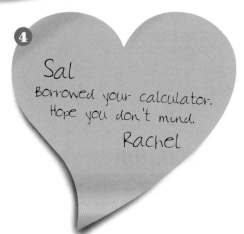

1
Martin
Gone to lunch - back in half an hour.
Document in C:\personal
Sal

2
Kerry
Boss phoned -
had to leave early!
Your sandwiches are
in fridge!
Mum

3
Pete
Great news! Would love to go.
See you at 7 at station.
Mark

4
Sal
Borrowed your calculator.
Hope you don't mind.
Rachel

7 Use these words to rewrite the four messages in Exercise 6 in full sentences.

1 I've/I'll be/Your/is
2 My/I/the
3 I/I'll/the
4 I've/I

8 In pairs, read Vicky's reply to Pete. Cross out any unnecessary words or phrases. Is there any missing information? Check your answers on page 141.

Dear Pete,

How's it going?

I am meeting my 19-year-old cousin from Bolton in Racey's on Saturday evening so I'm afraid I can't go with you, Mark and Rachel. What a pity – I haven't been to the theatre for ages.

Anyway, do you want to meet for a coffee on Sunday at about 3 o'clock? I will be upstairs in Toni's café – in the non-smoking area, of course.

Don't forget to let me know if there are any problems or if you can't come.

Best wishes,

Vicky XXX

9 Write a short note inviting a friend to one of the events from the arts festival leaflet on page 107. Use Speak Out and Train Your Brain to help you.

- Say which event it is.
- Suggest a time and a place to meet and something you could do afterwards.
- Mention how your partner can contact you if there is a problem.

10 Exchange your note from Exercise 9 with a partner, and write a reply. Use Speak Out on page 107 to help you.

VOCABULARY AND GRAMMAR

1 Put these words in the correct categories. Then add three more words from Units 11–12 to each group.

amazing   director   mugging   murderer
piracy   predictable   shoplifter
soundtrack   thriller   western

Criminals: _____ , _____ , _____ ,
_____ , _____

Crimes: _____ , _____ , _____ ,
_____ , _____

Film production: _____ , _____ ,
_____ , _____ , _____

Types of films: _____ , _____ ,
_____ , _____ , _____

Adjectives for films: _____ , _____ ,
_____ , _____ , _____

2 Match 1–8 with a–h to make collocations and compound nouns.

1 appear ☐   a a crime
2 break ☐   b dodging
3 cheat ☐   c hacking
4 commit ☐   d in an exam
5 computer ☐   e in court
6 fare ☐   f the law
7 private ☐   g property

3 Complete the sentences with the correct form of the words in capital letters.

1 I've seen a fascinating _____
of cinema posters.   EXHIBIT
2 I've got too much work. I need
a personal _____ .   ASSIST
3 Your _____ doesn't sound
convincing at all!   EXPLAIN
4 The writer complained that
he was _____ .   UNDERSTAND
5 It was _____ of you to
take that money.   HONEST
6 I always know what you are going
to do – you are so _____ !   PREDICT

4 Complete the sentences so that they have the same meaning as the original sentences.

1 'But Jane … Tom doesn't enjoy old movies!'
I told Jane that _____

_____ .

2 'The thieves have robbed four banks in one week!'
The police reported that the thieves _____

_____ .

3 'Mr. Cross. You murdered Ben Box!'
The lawyer said _____

_____ .

4 'You will never catch me!'
The man said that the police _____

_____ .

5 'Watson, the women aren't guilty!'
Sherlock Holmes told Dr Watson _____

_____ .

5 Read the email. For each gap circle the correct answer.

We're back home.

Reply   Reply All   Forward   Follow Up

From: julie@yes.com
To: ann@town.ox.uk
Subject: We're back home.

Hi, Ann,

At last we're back from our holidays! We got home early on ¹___ Saturday morning. We were all really tired because we ²___ all night. But when we opened ³___ front door, I couldn't believe my eyes. I ⁴___ anything like it before! Our house had been burgled! I immediately phoned our neighbours, ⁵___ Simpsons. They told me that the police ⁶___ a young man in our street. Later on, in ⁷___ afternoon we ⁸___ by ⁹___ young police officer. She ¹⁰___ us that we had forgotten to lock the back door!

Take care
Julie

1 a –   b a   c an   d the
2 a slept   b had slept
  c hadn't slept   d weren't sleeping
3 a –   b a   c an   d the
4 a never saw   b was never seen
  c was never seeing   d had never seen
5 a –   b a   c an   d the
6 a already caught   b caught already
  c had already caught d already had caught
7 a –   b a   c an   d the
8 a interviewed   b were interviewed
  c had interviewed   d have interviewed
9 a –   b a   c an   d the
10 a told   b was told
   c had told   d was telling

PRONUNCIATION

1 CD 3.18 Listen and circle the underlined letters which are pronounced with the sound /ə/. Which letters are usually pronounced as /ə/?

1 actor   6 fiction   11 library
2 amazing   7 frustration   12 mugger
3 cinema   8 graffiti   13 officer
4 computer   9 horror   14 romantic
5 exhibition   10 innocent   15 western

LISTENING SKILLS

1 **CD 3.19** Listen to the radio programme. Tick true and cross false.

1 Leslie Brown works on a gas platform. ☐
2 Leslie found a strange object on top of his wardrobe. ☐
3 He didn't hear the strange noises the thing made. ☐
4 The thing on his wardrobe was a Russian satellite. ☐
5 The thing was found by the police. ☐
6 Leslie had taken some radar equipment. ☐
7 The judge told Leslie to pay more than $2,000. ☐

READING SKILLS

1 Read the article and circle the correct answers.

The millionaire secretary

Criminal or hero?
In one of the most amazing financial scandals ever, Joyti De-Laurey, a secretary in a banking company, stole £4.5m from her employers in order to buy herself designer clothes, expensive cars and jewellery. She copied her bosses' signatures, wrote cheques to herself and stole the money from their personal bank accounts. Some people think she was a hero: a modern-day Robin Hood. Others say she was just an ordinary criminal.

Expensive tastes
The 37-year-old from London spent millions. She shopped in the most expensive shops, went to the best hairdressers and regularly ate in the most exclusive restaurants. She bought an Aston Martin car, a villa in Cyprus, and spent more than £350,000 on Cartier jewellery. The more money she spent, the fatter she got. By the time she had spent £4.5m, she was enormous and needed even more clothes in larger sizes.

Enormous salaries
Her bosses earned so much money that months went past before anybody noticed that she had stolen anything. One ex-managing director said, 'When you're making £60m a year, a few million missing is like a regular person not remembering the last penny on their account.'

You're under arrest
Finally De-Laurey was caught in May 2002. Her boss was going to give some money to charity, so he had checked his bank accounts and discovered that there was a fortune missing. The police found many expensive things in De-Laurey's house: Cartier jewellery still in its boxes, almost fifty designer handbags, and lots more. She never got to live in the dream villa she had bought in the Mediterranean. Unfortunately for her, she was arrested just before she left for Cyprus.

A great artist
During her trial she laughed and joked with the journalists who described her as the 'Picasso of Con Artists'. She said that her bosses had told her she could take the money. Unsurprisingly, the jury didn't believe her story, and she was found guilty. The judge said that she was a born liar and sentenced her to seven years in prison.

1 What was Joyti De-Laurey's job?
  a secretary
  b designer
  c banker

2 Who did she steal from?
  a her company
  b her bosses
  c exclusive shops

3 What happened to her because of her new lifestyle?
  a She lost weight.
  b She got fatter.
  c She moved to Cyprus.

4 Why did nobody notice what she was doing?
  a She was very careful.
  b She didn't steal much.
  c Her bosses had too much money.

5 How was she caught?
  a She told her boss what she was doing.
  b Her boss examined his bank account.
  c A policeman saw her with some jewellery.

6 What did she say at her trial?
  a That she was a great artist.
  b That she hadn't taken any money.
  c That her bosses had allowed her to take the money.

SPEAKING SKILLS

1 Roleplay the conversation.

Student A
You're on a language course in Liverpool. You are planning your Saturday afternoon with a friend from the course.
- Suggest what you can do (suggest the place and form of entertainment).
- Think for a moment but finally agree to the suggestion.
- Say that you hope you will enjoy what your friend suggests.
You start the conversation.

Student B
You're on a language course in Liverpool. You are planning your Saturday afternoon with a friend from the course.
- Disagree with your friend's suggestion, giving your reasons.
- Make your own suggestion.
- Tell your friend you are sure that he/she will enjoy what you have suggested and give the time of the meeting.
Student A starts the conversation.

Health matters

Read, listen and talk about health and sport.
Practise Second Conditional; modal verbs.
Focus on giving advice; dealing with new words in listening.
Write a letter giving advice.

If I'm not too tired, I'll do some ¹_____ tonight. And I'll go ²_____ on Sunday morning if Mum lends me the money.

I would try ³_____ and ⁴_____ if I didn't live so far from the coast. It must be great fun!

If the weather's nice, I'll play ⁵_____ with Becky. And if it rains, I'll go to the fitness club and do ⁶_____ for a couple of hours.

If I had the money, I would go ⁷_____. And I'd try ⁸_____ too if I wasn't so scared of heights!

GRAMMAR AND SPEAKING

1 In pairs, check these sports. Which sports can you see in the pictures above?

aerobics   bungee jumping   snowboarding
tennis   horse-riding   rock climbing
surfing   volleyball   kick boxing
scuba diving   swimming   weight training

2 In pairs, decide which of the sports in Exercise 1 are:

- team sports.
- indoor sports.
- martial arts.
- dangerous or extreme sports.
- outdoor sports.
- played with a racket.
- most popular in your country.

3 (CD 3.20) Listen to Scott and Danielle and complete the texts opposite (1–8) with the sports they mention.

4 **Think Back!** Look at the sentences below and circle the correct words in the rules.

I'll go swimming on Sunday morning if Mum lends me the money.
If the weather's nice, I'll play tennis with Becky.

- We use the First Conditional to talk about a realistic situation in the *past / future*.
- We use the *Present Simple / Past Simple* after *if*, and *will* in the other part of the sentence.

Work it out

5 Look at the sentences and answer the questions.

If I <u>had</u> the money, I <u>would go</u> snowboarding.
I <u>would</u> try surfing and scuba diving if I <u>didn't live</u> so far from the coast.

1 Do these sentences describe situations which are likely to come true in the future?
2 Which tense is used after *if* in these sentences?
3 Which verb is used before the infinitive in the other part of the sentence?

Check it out

The Second Conditional

We use the Second Conditional to talk about:

- a situation in the present that is unlikely or impossible to change.

If I **didn't live** so far from the coast, **I'd go** surfing more often. (but I live too far from the coast)

- an action that is unlikely to happen in the future. We often use it to talk about fantasies or unreal plans.

What sport **would** you **like** to do if you **had** the chance?
If I **had** the money, **I'd love** to try horse-riding. (but I don't have enough money)

The condition	The result
If + Past Simple,	*would* + infinitive

Mind the trap!

With the Second Conditional we often use *were* – instead of *was* – after *I*, *he*, *she* and *it*, especially in written English or formal situations.

I would go for a walk if **it weren't** so cold.
If **I were** you, I'd see a doctor.

6 Complete these Second Conditional sentences with the correct form of the verbs in brackets.

1 If I _____ (be) taller, I _____ (play) volleyball.
2 If she _____ (have) enough money, she _____ (join) the fitness club.
3 I _____ (take) some exercise if I _____ (be) you.
4 They _____ (go) hiking if they _____ (not have) exams at the moment.
5 If I _____ (be) fitter, I _____ (try) rock climbing.
6 If you _____ (play) sport more often, you _____ (not feel) so stressed out.
7 _____ (you/go) swimming more often if the swimming pool _____ (be) nearer?

7 In pairs, discuss which sports from Exercise 1 you would like to try. Make sentences using these ideas to help you.

- live nearer the mountains/the sea
- have enough money
- have someone to go with
- be braver/fitter/taller
- be better at …
- have more free time

If I was better at swimming, I'd love to try scuba diving.

8 First or Second Conditional? Complete the sentences with the correct forms of the verbs in brackets.

1 Life _____ (be) easier if everybody _____ (speak) English!
2 I _____ (make) boxing illegal if I _____ (be) President.
3 If my headache _____ (not get) better soon, I _____ (take) an aspirin.
4 It's a pity our team hasn't got any money – if we _____ (buy) a new goalkeeper, the team _____ (be) much stronger.
5 I _____ (go) cycling with you this weekend if my brother _____ (lend) me his bike.
6 You _____ (be) ill if you _____ (eat) all that chocolate cake!
7 I _____ (go) skiing if I _____ (live) nearer the mountains.

9 Work in groups. Choose one of the questions below, interview everyone in your group and then report your results.

- If you could be any famous sports star, who would you choose to be? Why?
- If a doctor told you that you had to lose weight and get fit, what would you do?
- If you had to take part in an extreme sport, which sport would you choose?

115

READING AND VOCABULARY

1 In pairs, look at the photos below and read the first paragraph of the text.

   1 What is special about Janek Mela?
   2 Why did he go to Antarctica?
   3 Why do you think his story is special?

2 `CD ROM` **Read the text and circle the correct answers.**

1 When the accident happened, Janek was:
   a with some school friends.
   b trying to avoid the rain.
   c going home.

2 Janek's parents contacted Marek Kamiński because they:
   a thought he could be an inspiration to Janek.
   b knew he had an ambitious idea.
   c wanted Janek to go to the North Pole.

3 Before the expedition Janek:
   a had to train very hard.
   b learnt to swim for the first time.
   c stopped studying.

4 During the expedition to the North Pole:
   a they couldn't walk very far some days.
   b they travelled at 2 km per hour.
   c they were lucky with the weather.

5 The trip to the South Pole
   a was easier than the trip to the North Pole.
   b began when Janek was fifteen.
   c was not a success.

6 After the expedition Janek
   a had completely changed.
   b was an inspiration to other young people.
   c joked about going on more expeditions.

A modest hero

In 2004, Janek Mela became the youngest person in history to ski unassisted to the North Pole. Six months later, Janek travelled to Antarctica with a new goal – to walk to the South Pole. An unbelievable challenge for any teenager. But for the people who knew Janek, his story was even more incredible.

1 The story really began in 2002, when Janek – who comes from Malbork in Poland – was thirteen years old. He was playing table tennis with some school friends when it suddenly started raining heavily. Most of Janek's friends ran home, but Janek and a friend decided to shelter from the storm in a small building. The building was actually an electricity substation and Janek suffered a shock of 15,000 volts. He lost his left arm and a leg in the accident.

3 Match phrasal verbs 1–5 with definitions a–e.

1 cheer someone up (para. 2) ☐
2 catch up with (para. 3) ☐
3 take up (para. 3) ☐
4 set out (para. 4) ☐
5 fall behind with (para. 6) ☐

a make less progress than other people
b make someone feel less sad
c reach the same level as other people
d start a (long) journey
e start a new sport or hobby

4 Complete the sentences with the correct form of the phrasal verbs from Exercise 3.

1 It was a long way to the next youth hostel so we _____ very early.
2 I was feeling a bit depressed so I ate some chocolate to _____ myself _____.
3 I was ill for three weeks so I _____ my studies, but I worked hard and soon _____ my classmates.
4 He wanted to lose weight so he decided to _____ jogging.

5 In pairs, check the meaning of the adjectives below. Choose three to describe Janek. Give reasons for your choices.

brave   modest   vain   talented
controversial   inspiring   confident
unambitious   unusual   independent

I think Janek is very brave. It's so difficult and dangerous to go to both Poles, especially if you're disabled.

6 Work in groups. Which of these things would you find the most challenging? Give reasons.

- go on an expedition to an extreme place
- give a speech in front of a crowd of 200 people
- go to another country to live
- live without music/television
- travel abroad alone

I would find it very stressful to give a speech in front of a lot of people. I'm quite shy.

2 Janek spent the next few months in hospital. His parents contacted the famous Polish explorer, Marek Kamiński, who was a family friend. They hoped that Marek could cheer Janek up and encourage him not to lose hope. But Marek came up with a much more ambitious idea – he wanted Janek to make a trek with him to the North Pole.

3 After he left hospital, Janek had to catch up with his schoolwork but he also began to train intensively for the expedition. Over the next year and a half, Janek had to learn to swim and ride a bike again. He also took up skiing, which he had never tried before.

4 In May 2004, Janek and Marek set out on the long walk to the North Pole. The weather was horrendous and often after a day's walking they were only two or three kilometres closer to the Pole than the previous day. But on 24 May Janek became the first disabled person to ski unassisted to the North Pole.

5 Janek's Antarctic expedition seven months later was even more challenging. Sometimes the temperature fell to minus thirty-five degrees and winds reached 100 km an hour. Janek celebrated his sixteenth birthday, 30 December 2004, in terrible conditions about thirteen kilometres from the South Pole. His birthday present was two bars of chocolate! But Janek finally reached the South Pole the next day and at the same time he broke another world record – the youngest person, and the first disabled person, to reach both the North and South Poles in the same year.

6 During his absence from Poland, Janek had become a hero – and not just to other disabled people. Many young people told Janek that his story had taught them that it was important to give yourself difficult goals in life. 'Sometimes suffering can destroy a person, and sometimes it can make him or her stronger,' says Janek's mother. Despite Janek's fame and success, he is still a modest schoolboy who worries that he has fallen behind with his schoolwork. But he is certain that he will make another expedition in the future – 'Perhaps Siberia is next,' he says. And he isn't joking.

Harry Uh! Darling! Could you come here, please?
Carol Do I have to? I'm watching television.
Harry Oh! Carol! Carol! Carol! I've got an awful pain in my chest. It says in my medical encyclopedia that the first signs of a heart attack are …
Carol You shouldn't read that book, Harry. It's probably just indigestion. You ate those sandwiches too quickly.
Harry But it's not just my chest. Feel my forehead. Maybe I've caught a dangerous virus too. And my throat is terribly red. Perhaps it's cancer of the …
Carol You've probably just got a cold and a sore throat. You should take an aspirin.
Harry An aspirin? What good's that going to do?
Carol My mother was right – Harry Hypochondriac she used to say. I'm going … I don't have to listen to this.

Harry Harry Hypochondriac indeed! I'm going to phone the doctor I am! Hello? Can I speak to Doctor Curtis, please? It's not possible?! But I must speak to him! Hello? Oh, Dr Curtis. Hello it's Harry Mac … Ah, you recognised me. I've got terrible pains in my … Oh?
Carol Well, what did he say?
Harry Dr Curtis says I have to stop reading my medical encyclopedia and …
Carol What else?
Harry He says that I mustn't phone him again!

GRAMMAR AND VOCABULARY

1 〔CD 3.21〕 In pairs, look at the cartoon. Why do you think the doctor is angry? Listen and check.

2 〔CD 3.21〕 Use a dictionary to check the meaning of the words below. Then read and listen to the conversation in Exercise 1 again. Tick the problems which Harry thinks he has.

a cold ☐   cancer ☐   indigestion ☐
a sore throat ☐   a temperature ☐
a dangerous virus ☐   a heart attack ☐

Work it out

3 Find verbs 1–6 in the conversation above. Then match them with their meanings a–f.

1 shouldn't ☐   a It's a good idea to …
2 should ☐   b It's not necessary to …
3 don't have to ☐   c I'm not allowed to …
4 must ☐   d It's not a good idea to …
5 have to ☐   e It's necessary to …
6 mustn't ☐   f It's necessary to …

Check it out

Modal verbs

- *must* and *have to* mean something is necessary
  I **must** phone the doctor.
  (It is necessary to phone him.)
  He says I **have to** exercise more.
  (He says it is necessary for me to exercise more.)

- *don't have to* means something isn't necessary
  I **don't have to** listen to this.
  (It isn't necessary for me to listen to this.)

- *mustn't* means something is not allowed
  You **mustn't** phone me.
  (You're not allowed to phone me.)

- *should* means something is a good idea
  You **should** take an aspirin. (It's a good idea to take an aspirin.)

- *shouldn't* means something isn't a good idea
  You **shouldn't** read that book. (It isn't a good idea to read that book.)

4 In pairs, read the advert and circle the correct answer.

Bad Cold? Headache? Sore throat?

- You *shouldn't / have to* stop eating.
- You *should / mustn't* have a lot of hot drinks.
- You *must / shouldn't* stay in bed if you've got a temperature.
- You *must / shouldn't* go to school or work.
- You *don't have to / must* see a doctor if you don't get better.

And remember to take Citrocon, available from all good chemists!

Citrocon

Mind the trap!

Must and *have to* both mean that *it is necessary to do something* but there is a difference between them.

Must means that the speaker personally feels that it is necessary to do something.
I **must** phone the doctor immediately!
(I feel absolutely terrible!)

Have to means it is necessary to do something because it's a rule/the law or somebody else told the speaker to do something.
The doctor says I **have to** give up smoking.

5 Complete the sentences with *must, mustn't, have to* or *don't have to*.

1 You _____ smoke in the hospital.
2 You _____ fill in all the form – your name and signature are enough.
3 I _____ remember to go to the chemist's. I've got a sore throat.
4 I feel fine but my doctor tells me that I _____ take more exercise.
5 Thanks but you really _____ help me – I can do it myself.
6 You _____ eat before your operation. It's dangerous!

6 Work in groups. Organise a sports camp for young people. Make a list of rules. Use the ideas below.

- Get up/Go to bed at …
- Keep quiet between … and …
- Smoke or drink alcohol
- Keep rooms clean
- Take part in all the activities
- Invite guests to the camp
- Stay with the group during trips/activities

You don't have to take part in all the activities.
You mustn't invite guests to the camp.

VOCABULARY

1 CD 3.22 Look at pictures a–f and match them with the words below. Then listen and check.

hay fever ☐   backache ☐
toothache ☐   a headache ☐
stomachache ☐   flu ☐

2 CD 3.23 In pairs, match problems 1–6 with the best advice a–f. Then listen and check.

1 toothache ☐
2 hay fever ☐
3 stomachache ☐
4 flu ☐
5 a headache ☐
6 backache ☐

a Drink some peppermint tea.
b Take a painkiller and lie down.
c Stay indoors.
d Phone for a doctor.
e Take an aspirin.
f See a dentist.

3 In pairs, give advice for each problem. Use the ideas below.

- a headache
- a temperature
- a stomachache
- flu
- hayfever
- backache

lie down   take an aspirin
drink lots of water   see a doctor
take antibiotics   stay in bed
go to school/work   ignore the problem
take some time off work   stop eating

A I've got a headache.
B You should take an aspirin.

119

LISTENING

1 [CD 3.24] Listen to the dialogue and answer the questions. Don't worry if you don't understand all the words.

- What's wrong with the patient?
- What are the reasons for his health problems?

2 [CD 3.24] Listen again to the context these words are used in. Then decide what part of speech each word is – noun (n), verb (v) or adjective (adj).

1 exhausted ☐   3 cope ☐
2 brisk ☐   4 booklet ☐

3 [CD 3.25] What do you think the words in Exercise 2 mean? Listen for clues before or after the words. Then, in pairs, choose the best definitions.

1 exhausted
  a very disappointed ☐
  b very tired ☐
  c very fit ☐

2 brisk
  a quick and energetic ☐
  b pleasant ☐
  c relaxing ☐

3 cope
  a increase ☐
  b manage ☐
  c invite ☐

4 booklet
  a exercise ☐
  b brochure ☐
  c medicine ☐

4 Read the sentences in Train Your Brain. Fill in the missing words. Look at Exercises 2 and 3 to help you.

TRAIN YOUR BRAIN | Listening skills

Dealing with new words

When you hear a word which you don't understand:
a analyse the context in which the word is used to decide what _____ it is.
b listen out for clues _____ or _____ the word to help you guess the meaning.

---

5 [CD 3.26] Listen to the dialogue and try and guess the meaning of the words below. Use Train Your Brain to help you.

hip   unbearable   prescription   swallow

6 [CD 3.26] Compare your answers to Exercise 5 with a partner. Listen again. Then check your answers in a dictionary.

SPEAKING AND WRITING

1 In pairs, answer the questions.

- Do you like Monday mornings? Why?/Why not?
- What is your typical Monday morning like? Describe your routine before you leave home.

2 [CD 3.27] Look at Dr Moody's advice and circle the ideas that you think are best for making Monday mornings more pleasant. Then listen and check.

Dr Moody's advice

1 _____ get up as late as possible. / an hour earlier than usual.

2 _____ listen to your favourite music. / do some housework.

3 _____ go for a walk. / do some work in the morning.

4 _____ do as little as possible. / plan to do something nice on Monday evenings.

5 _____ finish work as early as possible. / make a list of things to do during the next week.

3 *CD 3.27* Study Speak Out. Then listen again and fill in the expressions Dr Moody uses in the gaps in Exercise 2.

SPEAK OUT | Asking for and giving advice

Asking for advice
What should I do?
Could you give me some advice?
Have you any ideas about how to [+ *infinitive*]?
Have you any tips on how to ...?

Giving advice
If I were you, I'd ...
I (don't) think you should ...
You should/shouldn't ...
(I think) it's a good idea to ...
It's better (not) to ...
Why don't you [+ *infinitive*]?

Mind the trap!

Advice is uncountable, so it is always singular.

Can you give me some advice? NOT
~~Can you give me some advices?~~
~~Can you give me an advice?~~

4 Read the email to Becky from her classmates. What's the situation and what advice do you think she asked for? Circle the correct phrases.

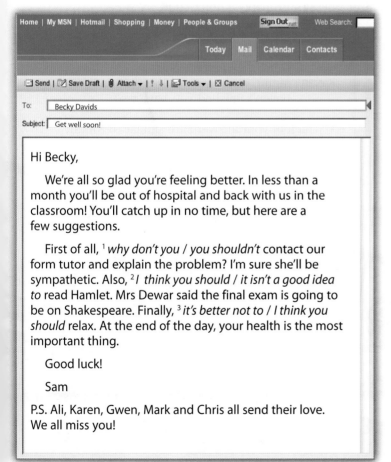

To: Becky Davids
Subject: Get well soon!

Hi Becky,

We're all so glad you're feeling better. In less than a month you'll be out of hospital and back with us in the classroom! You'll catch up in no time, but here are a few suggestions.

First of all, ¹ *why don't you / you shouldn't* contact our form tutor and explain the problem? I'm sure she'll be sympathetic. Also, ² *I think you should / it isn't a good idea to* read Hamlet. Mrs Dewar said the final exam is going to be on Shakespeare. Finally, ³ *it's better not to / I think you should* relax. At the end of the day, your health is the most important thing.

Good luck!

Sam

P.S. Ali, Karen, Gwen, Mark and Chris all send their love. We all miss you!

5 In pairs, give advice to your partner on one of the problems below.

- What to do on the evening before a big exam.
- Advice to help someone who has problems sleeping.
- How to keep fit if you don't have much time or money.

6 In pairs, roleplay the situation. Use phrases from Speak Out to help you.

Student A
It's your boyfriend/girlfriend's birthday soon and you don't have any ideas for a present. He/She hates clothes and jewellery but he/she is interested in art and music. Explain your problem to your friend and:
- ask him/her for some advice.
- thank your friend for his/her advice and tell him/her what you have decided to do.
- make some suggestions for your friend's problem.

Student B
Look at page 142 and start the conversation.

7 Write a short letter to a friend giving advice on one of the problems in Exercise 5. Use the ideas below to help you.

- Use the advice from Becky's friends in Exercise 4 and your advice from Exercise 5 to help you.
- Try to use as many different expressions from Speak Out as you can.
- Then swap letters with a friend. Is their advice useful?

121

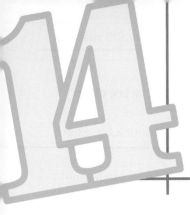

Europe, Europe

Read, listen and talk about Europe and the European Union.
Practise question tags.
Focus on talking about plans and intentions.
Write a formal letter giving information.

GRAMMAR AND LISTENING

1 Read the quiz below. Check any new words in a dictionary. Can you answer any of the questions?

2 **CD 4.1** Listen and write Kieran and Becky's answers to the quiz.

Internet Explorer

View Favorites Tools Help

Forward Stop Refresh Home Search Favorites History Mail Print Edit Links »

http://www1.allabouttheEU.org   Go

all about the EU

HOW MUCH DO YOU KNOW ABOUT THE EUROPEAN UNION? – TRY OUR INTERACTIVE QUIZ!

1 How many gold stars are on the EU flag?

2 Which country has the largest population in the EU?

3 Which composer's music was chosen for the EU anthem?

4 In which city does the European Parliament meet?

5 Which country isn't a member of the EU – Greece, Malta, Norway or Slovenia?

6 How many cents are in one euro?

Internet

---

3 **CD 4.1** Listen again and read the dialogue. Then in pairs, answer the questions.

Kieran Hey, Becky. Why don't we try this quiz on the European Union? Do you know the answer to the first question?

Becky Well, there are twenty-five countries in the EU, aren't there? So it must be twenty-five stars!

Kieran Well, I'm sure I know the answer to question two. It's Germany, isn't it?

Becky Yes … I think so.

Kieran Right – question three. Well, the European Union anthem is *Ode to Joy*. Was it composed by Mozart?

Becky No, Mozart didn't write it, did he? It was Beethoven!

Kieran Of course it was! This quiz isn't so easy, is it? Now question four. I'm not sure. The European Parliament meets in Brussels, doesn't it?

Becky Probably. I don't know.

Kieran OK, I'll write Brussels. What about question five? Malta?

Becky No, Malta joined in 2004, didn't it? I think the answer's Norway.

Kieran Mmm, you're right, I think. Oh no! We haven't finished yet, have we?

1 Which of your answers are similar to Kieran and Becky's?
2 Do you think any of their answers are wrong? Check on page 141.

Work it out

4 Look at the questions from the dialogue and circle the correct words in the rules below.

1 The European Parliament meets in Brussels, doesn't it?
2 Mozart didn't write it, did he?

a To make question tags we use the *auxiliary / main* verb and a pronoun.
b With *affirmative / negative* sentences we use an affirmative question tag.
c With *affirmative / negative* sentences we use a negative question tag.

5 Complete the sentences with the correct question tags. Use the dialogue in Exercise 3 to help you.

Question tags

We use question tags at the end of sentences when we are:

• unsure about what we are saying and we want the other person to confirm if we are right or not.
• sure and simply want the other person to agree with us.

There are twenty-five countries in the EU, aren't there?
The European Parliament meets in Brussels, _____ ?
Malta joined in 2004, _____ ?
This quiz isn't so easy, _____ ?
Mozart didn't compose it, _____ ?
We haven't finished yet, _____ ?

6 Complete the sentences with the correct question tag.

1 You haven't been to Brussels, _____ ?
2 The European Court is in Luxembourg, _____ ?
3 They use the euro in Spain, _____ ?
4 Britain joined the EU in 1973, _____ ?
5 Many British politicians didn't want to join the EU, _____ ?
6 The EU is getting bigger, _____ ?
7 Many people won't vote in the referendum, _____ ?
8 The EU was called the Common Market before, _____ ?

Mind the trap!

There are some irregular or unusual question tags.

I'm right, aren't I?
Nobody understands, do they?
Everybody understands, don't they?
Nobody is coming, are they?
Everybody is coming, aren't they?

7 Make a sentence using each question tag in the box. Then compare your answers with your partner.

..., aren't you?   ..., hasn't he?   It's ...
We'll ...   ..., did she?   Nobody ...
..., aren't I?   ..., have you?   Everybody ...

8 In pairs, use the statements below and question tags to make true sentences about the EU. Does your partner agree with you? Check your answers on page 141.
1 Switzerland is a member of the EU.
2 More countries will join the EU in the future.
3 There are ten cents in one euro.
4 EU citizens aren't allowed to work or study in other EU countries.
5 Luxembourg is the smallest country in the EU.
6 Spain joined the EU in 1986.
7 The euro has become the official currency in the UK.

A Switzerland isn't a member of the EU, is it?
B I think you're right but I'm not sure.

9 In pairs, check what you know about your partner. Make sentences with question tags about these topics.

countries visited   favourite band/singer
plans for the future   place of birth
number of brothers/sisters
hobbies/interests

A You've been to Turkey, haven't you?
B Yes, that's right.

OUR CRACOW, OUR COPENHAGEN

Danielle MacFarlane looks back at the unlikely birth of the European Union.

Today twenty-five countries belong to the European Union. More than 450 million Europeans have the right to live in, work in or travel to other EU countries. Millions of people enjoy friendly contact with their neighbours across borders. Governments across Europe pass the same laws about employment, food, transport, health and the environment. The EU is also the largest free market in the world. A typical European supermarket is full of fresh fruit, vegetables, cheese and meat which come from all over Europe. Twelve countries even use the same currency, the euro. In fact, the European Union has a very big influence over our lives, but most of us don't even notice it.

But if we look at Europe just three generations ago, we start to understand that the story of the EU is even more surprising. In 1945, Europe had just experienced the most terrible war in history. Many historians believe that at least forty million people were killed, although such numbers are very hard to calculate. At the end of the war millions were homeless and much of Europe was in ruins. In fact, famine was a bigger problem in 1947 than it was during the war years. Worst of all, many countries still didn't trust each other. It is perhaps a surprise to learn that the first politician to suggest 'a United Europe' after the war was Winston Churchill, the British Prime Minister during the war years. In September 1946, during a meeting in Switzerland, he said that Europeans should come together to create a 'United States of Europe'.

Modest beginnings. Six countries sign the Treaty of Rome in 1957

READING AND LISTENING

1 In pairs, answer the questions.

- Is your country a member of the EU?
- If yes, when did your country join?
- If no, would you like your country to join in the future?

2 Check you understand these words. Use a dictionary if you need to.

a law   a border   a currency   trade
a speech   a treaty

3 Quickly read the text 'Our Cracow, Our Copenhagen'.

1 How many countries have the same currency?
2 Who suggested a 'United States of Europe'?
3 When was the Treaty of Rome signed?

4 **CD ROM** Put the events in the correct order. Then read the text again and check your answers.

A major conference is organised.	☐
Churchill suggests 'a United States of Europe'.	☐
Schuman tries to keep the idea of cooperation alive.	☐
The EEC becomes the EU.	☐
The EEC is created.	☐
The Second World War ends.	☐

5 Read the text again. Tick true and cross false. Then correct the wrong sentences.

1 Not all EU countries have introduced the euro.
2 Hunger was a big problem in Europe, even two years after the end of the war.
3 Some countries didn't have a good relationship with each other after the war.
4 Churchill's ideas about 'a United Europe' were very popular.
5 The Netherlands conference was a success.
6 De Madariaga's vision has become reality.

However, most people, especially in Britain, thought that Churchill's ideas were shocking or even absurd. Eight months later a huge conference was organised in the Netherlands. Eight hundred important European academics and politicians were invited. Perhaps the most powerful speech was made by Salvador de Madariaga, a Spanish politician and writer:

This Europe must be born. And she will, when Spaniards say 'our Chartres', Englishmen say 'our Cracow', Italians 'our Copenhagen' and Germans 'our Bruges'. Then Europe will live.

But when de Madariaga spoke these words in 1947, it was already too late. Despite the fine words and emotional speeches, the Netherlands conference couldn't save Europe – it was already divided in two. But the idea of 'a United Europe' didn't die completely. A French politician, Robert Schuman, believed that the only way that France and Germany could become good neighbours again was by cooperating economically. In 1951, six countries agreed to regulate trade, prices and production of coal and steel. The experiment was a success, and in 1957 the six countries signed the Treaty of Rome and created the European Economic Community (in 1993, the EEC changed its name to the European Union). Nine more countries joined the organisation between 1973 and 1992 and another ten countries became members in 2004. Perhaps De Madariaga's dream will come true one day after all.

6 CD 4.2 Listen and decide which speakers have negative opinions about the EU. Then listen again and match speakers 1–5 with opinions a–e.

Speaker 1 ☐
Speaker 2 ☐
Speaker 3 ☐
Speaker 4 ☐
Speaker 5 ☐

a The EU sometimes seems to waste money.
b It makes Europe more democratic and peaceful.
c Too many decisions are made for us without consultation.
d It makes it easier for young people to travel and study abroad.
e It makes Europe more competitive economically.

7 In pairs, answer the questions.

• Do you think the EU is a good thing?
• Which of the opinions from Exercise 6 do you agree with most?

VOCABULARY

1 In pairs, complete the fact box with the missing words below.

capital   flag   national anthem   currency   government   population

! **The United Kingdom** – factbox

The UK FACTBOX

• 1 _____   60 million
• 2 _____   London
• 3 _____   God Save the Queen
• 4 _____   Red, white and blue
• Type of 5 _____   (Constitutional monarchy)/ Republic
• Member of the EU   (Yes)/ No
• Year of joining the EU   1973
• 6 _____   pound sterling (£)

Mind the trap!

We always use the singular of words like *hundred*, *thousand* or *million* after numbers.

The population of the UK is about sixty **million**. NOT sixty millions
Scotland has been part of the UK for about three **hundred** years. NOT three hundreds

2 In pairs, write a factbox for your country. Use the box in Exercise 1 to help you.

3 Match the verbs and phrases. One verb is used twice.

1 become ☐   a a law
2 have ☐ ☐   b a treaty
3 make ☐   c a member of (the EU)
4 pass ☐   d the right (to do something)
5 sign ☐   e a speech
   f an influence (on something)

4 Think Back! Reorder the words in capitals.

1 In Britain, the Prime Minister is the leader of the OMGENVRETN.
2 After the war, five countries signed a peace ATTREY.
3 Sweden and China want to increase RETAD between the two nations.
4 Politicians clapped after the ambassador's PESCHE.
5 There has been a long debate in RAMPILANET about identity cards.
6 Germany is a BEERMM of the European Union.

4 **CD 4.3** Listen again and circle the correct answer.

1 The European Broadcasting Union
  a produced twenty TV programmes.
  b cooperates with twenty other organisations.
  c came up with the idea of Eurovision.

2 Today, Eurovision
  a doesn't have as many countries as before.
  b is still very popular.
  c is watched by a billion Europeans.

3 Jacqueline thinks that Eurovision songs often
  a copy melodies from previous years.
  b have very serious texts.
  c are very short.

4 Abba and Celine Dion are artists who
  a copied somebody else's song.
  b sang for countries where they weren't born.
  c became better known after Eurovision.

5 Martin thinks that
  a Eurovision has helped to make Europeans
    understand one another.
  b certain countries vote in a very
    predictable way.
  c music is more important than politics.

6 Ireland is perhaps the most successful
  country in Eurovision because
  a it is popular with other European countries.
  b they always sing in English.
  c the UK doesn't do very well.

LISTENING

1 Do you know any famous singers or bands who have
taken part in Eurovision?

2 In pairs, look at the photos and try and guess which
decades these artists took part in Eurovision.

  1 ☐   2 ☐   3 ☐

  a 1960s   b 1970s   c 1980s

3 **CD 4.3** Listen and decide which sentence best
summarises the conversation.

  a Eurovision is a great television tradition
    which brings Europe closer together.
  b Eurovision is harmful and shouldn't be
    allowed.
  c The music is often terrible and the
    competition is often dominated by politics but
    it's very entertaining television.

5 In pairs, answer the questions.

  • Do you watch Eurovision?
  • Does your country take part? Has it ever won?
  • Do you think Eurovision is a good idea?
  • What other events are there where European
    countries compete against each other? Do
    you enjoy them?

SPEAKING AND LISTENING

1 `CD 4.4` Listen and look at the picture. Try to decide what the situation is.

2 `CD 4.5` Listen to the rest of the conversation and complete the table with the speakers' plans and intentions.

travel for a year   get to know relatives
become a diplomat   open a shop

	For the near future	In the long term
Anna		
Ryan		

3 `CD 4.5` Study Speak Out. Then listen again and tick the phrases you hear.

SPEAK OUT | Talking about wishes, plans and intentions

Plans for the near future	Plans in the long term
I'm going to	My ambition is to ... .
I'm planning to	My biggest dream is to ... .
I want to	I'd ..., if I had the chance.
If I ..., I'll	I would (really) love to ... .

4 `CD 4.5` Listen again and complete the gaps in the dialogue with phrases from Speak Out.

Pali So, Anna. What are your plans?

Anna What, you mean for the next few months? Well [1]_____ spend the summer in Poland. My family is from there and I've never been there before. I've got a cousin in Warsaw who's my age and [2]_____ meet him for the first time.

Ryan Sounds cool …

Anna And then, if my exam results are OK …

Pali If! Anna, you were the best student!

Anna If I pass my A-levels, [3]_____ study International Law at Kingston University.

Ryan Oooh! That sounds fun! And then what?

Anna Well, in the long term, I suppose [4]_____ work as a diplomat. What about you, Ryan?

Ryan Well, [5]_____ take a break for a while. Travel for a year around Europe. It's so easy these days. And then I'm going to study German at university.

Pali German? And what are you going to do with a German degree?

Ryan Oh, nothing probably. [6]_____ start my own business – but nothing too big. [7]_____ open my own skate shop – you know, skateboards, clothes, accessories … What's so funny about that? Anyway, Pali, what about your plans?

5 Tell your partner about your plans for the next few months and your long term plans. Use the words and phrases below and Speak Out to help you.

study   win   visit/see   pass   start a family
work as a …   improve   move to   earn
be a famous …   become the best …
take up   start my own …   buy/own a …
become an expert in …   get married

A I'd love to win a black belt in karate.
B If I had the chance, I'd love to study at a French university.

6 Student A, look at page 141. Student B, look at page 142. Then follow the instructions.

WRITING

1 In pairs, read Douglas's letter and answer the questions.

- Where does Douglas Campbell come from?
- Where do you think Ms Kralova comes from?
- When is Ms Kralova's school going to visit?
- What will the weather probably be like?
- Does Douglas know Ms Kralova well? How do you know?

inverness
THE CITY in THE HIGHLANDS

Invergordon High School

Invergordon High School
17 Blackwood Road
Invergordon
IV18 9GK

7th June, 2006

Dear Ms Kralova,

1 Thank you for your letter. I am writing on behalf of Invergordon High School's exchange committee. We are very pleased that you have agreed to take part in the exchange programme with our school this autumn. I hope to answer some of your questions in this letter.

2 You asked about the places we are going to visit during the two weeks. The nearest large town is Inverness. Perhaps it isn't as big and beautiful as Prague, but there's a lot to see. We also hope to visit Loch Ness – it's very near and the scenery is really beautiful. Invergordon is on the coast so there are a lot of pleasant seaside walks. There's an interesting old port in the town too.

3 You also asked what kind of clothing your students should take with them. September is usually quite warm (for Scotland…), but it does rain quite often. We're also going to do a lot of walking, so it is a good idea for students to bring some walking boots and waterproof jackets. Please remember to tell the students that they will need a passport or ID card to come to the UK.

4 Please find enclosed the planned timetable for the two weeks. We are really looking forward to seeing you all on September 25th. Please feel free to contact me if you have any other questions.

Yours sincerely,

Douglas Campbell

Douglas Campbell

2 **In pairs, match each paragraph with its subject.**

Para. 1 ☐   Para. 2 ☐
Para. 3 ☐   Para. 4 ☐

a Final greetings and offer to give more help or information
b Who the author of the letter is and his/her reason for writing
c Answer to the second enquiry (information about what to bring)
d Answer to the first enquiry (plans and places worth visiting)

3 **In pairs, look at the letter in Exercise 1 again and follow the instructions.**

1 Underline the sentences below that you would normally write in a formal letter.
2 Decide which of the underlined sentences usually go:
  • in the first paragraph of a letter.
  • in the last paragraph of a letter.

Say *hi* to your sister from me!
I hope to answer some of your questions.
Thank you for your letter.
Please feel free to contact me if you have any questions.
I am writing on behalf of …
Please find enclosed a map of how to find us.
How's it going?
We're/I'm looking forward to seeing you.
Write back soon!
Sorry, I haven't written for ages.

First paragraph	Last paragraph

4 Study Train Your Brain and check your answers to Exercise 3.

TRAIN YOUR BRAIN | Writing skills

A formal letter giving information

• In the first paragraph, thank your correspondent for a previous letter, explain who you are (*I am writing on behalf of …*) or why you are writing.
• In the next paragraphs answer your correspondent's questions and give more information. Use phrases like *we hope to/are going to, should/shouldn't, it's a good idea to, please remember to* etc. to talk about plans and arrangements.
• You can end the letter by inviting the person to write with more questions, and by saying that you hope to see or hear from him/her soon.
• If you are sending extra information like a map with your letter, use a phrase like *Please find enclosed …* .
• Remember to use formal style.

---

5 In pairs, what city or region in your country would you recommend to a visitor? Write sentences using the ideas below to help you.

beautiful scenery   sightseeing
very famous   a great atmosphere   relaxing
good for walking/sailing   a historic city
has an interesting history
a lot to see and do   good nightlife
very cheap   close/easy to travel to

Vilnius is a historic city with a lot to see and do.

6 Follow the instructions to write a letter giving information. Use Train Your Brain and your ideas from Exercise 5 to help you.

A class of students from the UK is coming to your school on an exchange programme. The form tutor, Mrs Cowan, wrote with some questions. Reply to her letter on behalf of the school organising committee. Answer the following questions:
• What towns and country regions are the students going to visit?
• Do students need visas to enter your country?
• Is it a good idea to bring an International Student Identity Card (ISIC)?
• Can they contact you if they need any further information?

VOCABULARY AND GRAMMAR

1 Complete the sentences. For each gap write one word. The first letter of each word is given.

1 If you've got toothache, take a **p**_____ and go and see a **d**_____ .
2 I've got a high **t**_____ , a terrible **h**_____ and a **s**_____ throat. Maybe I've got the flu.
3 I've joined a gym. I do **a**_____ . I also do **w**_____ **t**_____ to build up my muscles and I'm going to take up a **m**_____ **a**_____ like judo or maybe **k**_____ **b**_____ .
4 He's really keen on mountain sports: **r**_____ **c**_____ in the summer and **s**_____ in the winter.

2 Circle the correct word.

1 The government should hold a *law / referendum / treaty* on the new car tax.
2 A *democrat / diplomat / historian* must know how to talk to angry people.
3 I think the French national *anthem / border / flag* – the Marseillaise – is the best in the world.
4 She's so *competitive / modest / stressed out*. She's won three gold medals and she wants more.
5 I'm going to university to do a *degree / enquiry / programme* in international trade.
6 Why are you so sad? *Cheer / Call / Take* up a bit. It's not the end of the world.

3 Complete the second sentence so that it has a similar meaning to the first sentence. Use the word in bold and other words to complete each sentence.

1 My advice to you is not to sign it.
   I
   If _____
   not sign it.
2 I think she really likes him.
   she
   She really likes him, _____ ?
3 You are not allowed to visit me any more.
   visit
   You _____ me any more.
4 I don't think they have finished yet.
   they
   They haven't finished yet, _____ ?
5 I don't understand so I can't explain it to you.
   would
   If I _____ it to you.
6 If you work hard, you will soon be as good as the rest of the class.
   up
   If you work hard, you will soon _____ with the rest of the class.

4 Complete the sentences so that they have the same meaning as the original sentences.

1 They aren't brave. They won't go on an expedition to the South Pole.
   If they _____ .
2 You eat too much so you don't lose any weight.
   If you _____ .
3 She's thinking of taking up yoga because she feels stressed out.
   If she _____ .
4 Perhaps my mum will give me the money next week. I don't want to borrow it from my friend.
   If my mum _____ .
5 He has a sore back. He can't play football.
   If he _____ .

5 Complete the dialogue with the correct question tags or modal verbs.

Dorothy Helen, you're looking tired. Things aren't going well, [1]_____ ?
Helen No, I feel terrible.
Dorothy How come? You haven't fallen in love, [2]_____ ?
Helen No, I'm really tired at the moment. I just [3]_____ sleep at night.
Dorothy You [4]_____ join a gym or something.
Helen Hmm, maybe. But that takes up so much time, [5]_____ ? I suppose it would be a good idea though. All my summer clothes are too small for me. I've put on a lot of weight.
Dorothy Hey! You [6]_____ get depressed! It doesn't help at all, [7]_____ ? If you want to lose weight, it's simple. You [8]_____ go on a diet.
Helen That's alright for you to say. You don't have to watch what you eat, [9]_____ ?
Dorothy Hey! It's not my fault you're depressed.
Helen Yeah, I'm sorry. Listen, you haven't got any chocolate, [10]_____ ?

PRONUNCIATION

1 CD 4.6 Listen and put the words in the box in the correct columns. Then listen and check.

/ð/	/θ/
brother	anthem

both   north   other   than   thank   there
thing   birthday   together   tooth
weather   without

READING SKILLS

1 Read the article. Tick true and cross false.

1 The Euroscola day takes place several times a year. ☐
2 Every member country of the EU delegates 500 students to participate in the Euroscola programme. ☐
3 The day is always organised in Brussels. ☐
4 Although the participants speak different languages, there are no communication problems. ☐
5 The only official language is English. ☐
6 The students split into five big groups to discuss European issues. ☐
7 During the Euroscola day the students act in the same way as MEPs. ☐

Euroscola
– a day at the European Parliament

Twelve times a year, the Euroscola programme brings together a group of about five hundred 16–18-year-old secondary school students from fifteen European Union countries. They have a day of meetings in Strasbourg (and occasionally in Brussels) in order to learn about the European Parliament and to take part in presentations and discussions and to vote on European issues.

The students come from different cultures and countries but they all understand each other – although it is a multilingual experience, everyone can communicate in either French or English.

The day is led by officials of the Parliament who make sure that all the young people participate fully in the meetings. The students are divided into five working parties of about a hundred members. Each working party chooses a spokesperson to present the conclusions of its discussions to all five hundred participants at the end of the afternoon.

Although the students are quite young they are treated exactly as if they were Members of the European Parliament (MEPs): they sit in the main debating room, use electronic voting and so on. All the participants enjoy the experience, but young people who are self-confident and who are willing to speak in public probably benefit the most.

If you would like to receive more details about the programme or express an interest in participating, please contact the European Parliament.

SPEAKING SKILLS

1 Describe the photo. Then answer the questions.

1 Why do you think the people decided to take up this sport?
2 Do you think sports like this one make people more or less violent?

2 Roleplay the conversation.

Student A
You are an English-speaking tourist who is planning a holiday in your partner's country. You are going to visit your friend in his/her city.
- Tell him/her about your travel plans – when you are going, how long you are going to stay, who you are going with.
- Ask him/her about the best way to travel and where to stay.
- Tell him/her about what you would like to do while you are there and ask him/her for any advice.
You start the conversation.

Student B
A friend of yours is planning a holiday in your country. He/she is going to visit your city.
- Ask him/her about his/her travel plans.
- Suggest the best way to get to your city and a good place to stay.
- Give him/her some advice on how to have a good time in your city without spending too much money.
Your partner starts the conversation.

CULTURE SHOCK 1

EDUCATION IN ENGLAND

Glossary attend school bachelor's degree compulsory corporal punishment gap year nursery school/playgroup optional P.E. pre-school education punishment school uniform specialise

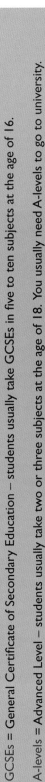

The School System

Typical Age	Type of Education	Type of School	School Years and Exams
3–4	**Pre-School Education** This is not compulsory, but 47 percent of children attend.	Nursery school/Playgroup	
4/5–10	**Primary Education**	Primary School	Year 1–Year 6
11–18	**Secondary Education** Students can leave school after Year 11 (16 years old) but more than 50 percent continue education for another two years (Years 12 and 13).	Secondary School (usually comprehensive schools, which are for students of all abilities.) Some students choose to study for their A-levels at a College of Further Education.	Year 7–Year 11 GCSEs Year 12–Year 13 A-levels
19–22	**Higher Education** About 40 percent of 19-year-olds enter higher education.	University (three or four years which finish with a Bachelor's degree – many students take a break (a gap year) before they start university.	

Exams

GCSEs = General Certificate of Secondary Education – students usually take GCSEs in five to ten subjects at the age of 16.

A-levels = Advanced Level – students usually take two or three subjects at the age of 18. You usually need A-levels to go to university.

1 In pairs, look at the table and answer the questions.

1 How old are children in Britain when they start their education?
2 At what age can they legally finish their education?
3 How many years of compulsory education do students have before they take their school-leaving exams (A-levels)?
4 How old are most students when they finish university?

2 CD 4.7 Listen to five school-leavers talking about British secondary-school life. Match the speakers with the topics. There are two answers that you don't need.

1 Frank ☐
2 Kirsty ☐
3 Jo ☐
4 Rob ☐
5 Naomi ☐

a The school day
b Physical Education (P.E.)
c Different types of school
d School uniform
e School clubs and societies
f Punishments
g Subjects

3 CD 4.7 Read the text and circle the correct words. Then listen and check your answers.

14 | education

>> School life

Some aspects of school life date back to the nineteenth century. One example is the school assembly, a meeting of the whole school every morning be-fore classes. Another is school uniform, which is still very common – about [1] *15 percent / 50 percent* of pupils in England wear school uniform.

The school day in both primary and secondary schools is fixed – the first lesson begins at 9.15a.m. and classes end at [2] *2.30p.m. / 3.30p.m.* every day. Classes on Saturdays are very unusual.

Compared with many countries, pupils in Britain specialise quite early. Pupils study many subjects until the age of fourteen, but then they usually study only three subjects during the last [3] *two / three years of school.*

Sport is an important part of school life. P.E. is compulsory. Typically boys play football or rugby in winter and cricket in spring; and girls usually do aerobics or play [4] *basketball / netball.*

Britain was one of the last countries to use corporal punishment in schools (it only became illegal in 1985). Nowadays teachers can punish their students with lines or detention, which means that students have to [5] *stay after school / do extra homework.*

4 In pairs, look at your answers to Exercise 3. How is life in British schools different from your country?

5 Crossing Cultures Discuss these questions in pairs. Use your answers to Exercises 1 and 4 and the ideas below to help you.

'Is there anything in the British education system that you think is a particularly good or bad idea compared with your country? Why?'

too old/young liberal long/short childhood a big/small percentage strict fair/unfair a large/small choice of subjects optional/compulsory start your first job more exams specialise early/late mature/immature

A I think school uniform is a good idea. You don't have to worry about wearing really fashionable clothes every day.
B I think children in Britain are too young when they start school. Their childhood is really short!

133

CULTURESHOCK2

ALTERNATIVE LONDON

Glossary breathtaking docks historic hustle and bustle market square medieval observatory skyscraper temple trendy

1 Read the Factbox about London. In pairs, write a similar box about your country's capital city.

2 Read the descriptions of the places on the map. Which place sounds the most interesting to visit? Why?

London CITYGUIDES

London – factbox

!

Population
about 7 million (about twelve percent of the UK population)

Location
southeast England on the River Thames

Became capital
in the ninth century

Most popular tourist destinations
Big Ben and the Houses of Parliament, Westminster Abbey, Buckingham Palace, Oxford Street, the Tower of London

Most famous art galleries and museums
the National Gallery, the Tate Galley, the British Museum, the Natural History Museum

Camden Lock
One of the liveliest parts of London. Young people come here from all over the world to buy unusual clothes and records, listen to music or even get a piercing or tattoo.

Hampstead
A district in the north of London. It's only five miles from the city centre but is famous for its quiet, village atmosphere. It's the home of many actors, writers and rock musicians.

Parliament Hill
When you walk up Parliament Hill, you feel as if you're far from the crowds and noise of the city. Your reward when you get to the top – a breathtaking view of central London.

Greenwich

Across the river from the commercial skyscrapers in the Docklands is historic Greenwich. The district has many handsome old buildings, the famous observatory from where we calculate all the world's time zones, interesting walks along the Thames and wonderful views of the city.

Whitechapel

A few years ago this was a poor district of East London. Now it's a fashionable place to work or go out clubbing. Many young artists have their studios here and it is the techno capital of the UK.

Soho

Not far from the tourist attractions of Trafalgar Square and Piccadilly Circus is Soho. The district has an exotic atmosphere with many alternative bars and cafés. It is also the centre of the UK music industry, so it's a good place to go shopping for CDs.

Southall

In the west of London, many people call it 'the Little Punjab'. When you walk down the busy streets full of exotic smells and colours, or see the beautiful Gurdwara (Sikh temple), you can really believe you are in India.

LONDON'S BEST-KEPT SECRETS?

Some of the most interesting things to see in London are far from the hustle and bustle of the city centre. Read our *Insider Guide* and discover some of the most interesting places that tourists rarely get to.

Historic places: old town walls   castle/palace   market square   old buildings   church   synagogue   cathedral   old town   docks

Other places to visit: museums   clubs   shops/boutiques   art galleries   cafés

Natural attractions: walks along the river   park   forest/wood   a wonderful view   hill   a path through/along

Adjectives: exciting   exotic   fashionable/trendy   gothic/classical   historic   lively   medieval   peaceful   relaxing

3   [CD 4.8] **In pairs, decide which places are the most interesting for the people below. Then listen and check your answers.**

1 Tomas is interested in different cultures.
2 Maria is interested in music, fashion and nightlife.
3 Miriam likes peace and quiet.
4 Evan is interested in history.

4   **Crossing cultures Work in groups. Answer the questions using the prompts below.**

1 Imagine that Tomas, Maria, Miriam and Evan are visiting your town or nearest city. What places or districts could they visit?
2 Write a few sentences for each visitor using the ideas below to help you.

A *Miriam could visit the Tiergarten because it's a park which is really relaxing to walk through in the evenings.*

CULTURE **SHOCK** 3

THE MONARCHY

Glossary abdicate boo divided family tree honourable the Industrial Revolution infamous monarch
pathetic Prince of Wales ruler support throne World War One ultimatum

Memorable MONARCHS

Today's royal family, the Windsors, have a family tree that goes back to the eleventh century. The function of the monarchy has changed much over the past 300 years – today Britain is a constitutional monarchy, which means that the government rules the country in the Queen's name. There is even a debate about whether Britain now needs its monarchy. However, there is no doubt that Britain's kings and queens have had a huge influence on British history and identity. Here are three particularly memorable monarchs.

❀ EDWARD VIII ❀

As Prince of Wales, Edward fought during World War One. He was worried by the revolutions at the end of the war when Germany and Russia lost their kings. Edward realised that the monarchy had to be close to the nation to survive. During the economic crisis of the 1930s he worked to help the unemployed. When he finally became king in 1936, he was perhaps the most popular monarch in British history. But he was also in love with an American woman, Wallis Simpson, who was still married. The government presented Edward with an ultimatum – either the throne or Mrs Simpson. On December 11 1936 Edward shocked the nation by telling them that he had abdicated. He had been king for less than eleven months. Edward married Mrs Simpson in 1937 and the couple spent the rest of their lives abroad.

❀ ELIZABETH I ❀

When Elizabeth became Queen in 1558, England was a weak, divided country. But during the 45 years she was in power, Elizabeth brought her nation together and England's position became stronger. It was a golden age – the age of Shakespeare and the voyages of discovery. Elizabeth was not a beautiful woman – she started going bald when she was quite young – but she had a magnetic personality and chose talented men to be her ministers. She once said that although she had the body of a woman, she had the heart and stomach of a king. Elizabeth never married – she used to say that her love affair was with the nation.

GEORGE IV

ELIZABETH

❖ GEORGE IV ❖

The beginning of the 19th century was an exciting time in Britain. Industry was growing and every year brought new technological innovations. There was a revolution in the arts too – this was the era of the Romantic poets and writers. It's a pity that one of the most hopeless kings in British history sat on the throne at the time. During the decade he ruled, he became famous for spending public money to support his expensive habits. He often didn't get up until six in the evening and was so large that he needed five men and a special ladder to help him get onto his horse. In fact, his reputation was so awful that British people booed and laughed at him when he appeared in public.

EDWARD VIII

1 **Quickly read the text and answer the questions.**

Which monarch:
1 lived in the 20th century?
2 was on the throne at the start of the Industrial Revolution?
3 lived at the same time as Shakespeare?

2 **Read the sentences and match them with a monarch from Exercise 1.**

1 He/She spent a lot of money on himself/herself. ____
2 He/She was in power for a long time. ____
3 He/She decided that love was more important than power. ____
4 He/She worried about the future of the monarchy. ____
5 He/She was very unpopular with the British people. ____
6 He/She was good at choosing government ministers. ____

3 **Which words do you think best describe each monarch? In pairs, choose two words for each person. Then compare your answers with another pair.**

Elizabeth I: ____
George IV: ____
Edward VIII: ____

respected   irresponsible   unpopular   strong   romantic   intelligent   lazy   caring   brave   honourable   pathetic   intriguing   loyal   popular   infamous

4 CD 4.9 **Listen to the programme about Elizabeth I. Which adjectives from Exercise 3 does Jill use to describe her? Were any of your adjectives the same?**

5 **Crossing Cultures Work in groups and note down your answers to these questions. Then compare your ideas with another group. Were any rulers chosen by more than one group?**

• Choose one famous ruler (a monarch, prime minister or president) in your country's history. When was he/she in power?
• What sort of reputation and personality did this person have? Use the words in Exercise 3 to help you.
• What makes him/her a memorable ruler? Use the ideas below to help you.

married/was in love with   argued with   encouraged   built/started   won/lost ... against ...   killed/was killed   changed   introduced   ended

CULTURESHOCK4

>> Places to visit in Britain

Bath

☐ A town not far from Bristol, this is one of England's most attractive cities. It contains some of the finest Roman buildings in Britain, including the famous baths which were built in 60AD. In the 18th century it became the most fashionable spa town in Britain. Today you can still see many streets of elegant terraced houses. It is a UNESCO World Heritage Site.

Canterbury

☐ A historic city in southeast England. In 597AD it was the place where St. Augustine introduced Christianity to England. The current cathedral was started in 1070. Canterbury is the home of the Archbishop of Canterbury, the head of the Anglican Church. In the 13th and 14th centuries thousands of pilgrims came to the town every year. This inspired Geoffrey Chaucer to write twenty-four stories about pilgrims travelling to Canterbury from London, one of the first masterpieces of English literature. Although Canterbury was damaged during World War Two, it still has many attractive medieval buildings and narrow streets.

Edinburgh

☐ The capital of Scotland. The centre of the city is full of historic medieval buildings, churches, palaces and museums. It is especially famous for its castle (12th century) which stands high over the city on a granite rock. It is an important university centre and is a centre for the arts. The arts festival which takes place here in August is the largest in Europe.

FAMOUS PLACES IN BRITAIN

Glossary ancient monument baths birthplace current guided tour pilgrim spa town stone circle world-famous

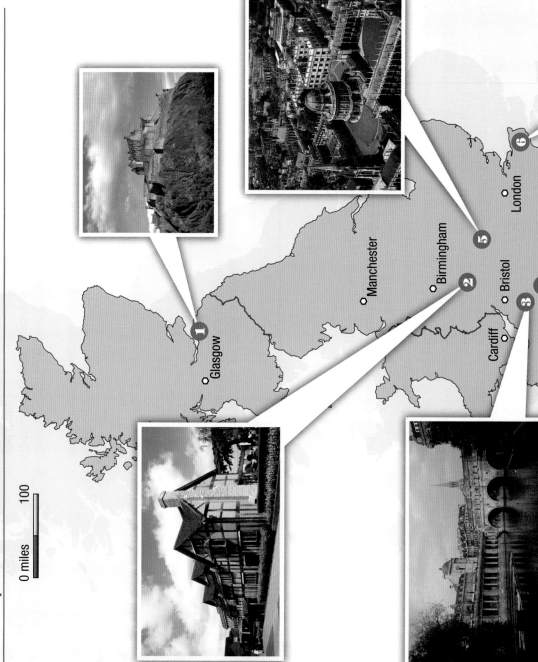

0 miles   100

Glasgow

Manchester

Birmingham

Cardiff

Bristol

London

1 2 3 4 5 6

Oxford

A city about fifty miles northwest of London. Its world-famous university was started in the 12th century – one of the first in Europe. The university has over thirty colleges but perhaps the most famous include Merton, Balliol and University College. In the 20th century it also became England's main centre for making cars. However, education still dominates Oxford – in fact eight percent of the population are teachers!

Stonehenge

A world-famous stone circle about 130 miles southwest of London. It was begun in about 3000BC and finished in about 1500BC. Some of the huge stones were brought from the Welsh mountains, hundreds of miles away. Nobody really knows exactly why it was built. One theory says that it was a kind of temple; another theory is that it was built to observe the stars.

Stratford-on-Avon

Stratford is a market town a little to the south of Birmingham. It is most famous for being the birthplace of William Shakespeare. Every year Stratford is visited by over two million tourists. Today it is an important cultural centre (the town is the home of the Royal Shakespeare Theatre).

enjoy**Britain**.com.uk

---

1 Quickly read the texts and match each place in the text with points 1–6 on the map.

2 Read the texts again and answer the questions. Sometimes there is more than one answer.

Which place:
1 is a university city?
2 has got a famous castle?
3 is the birthplace of someone famous?
4 has got a lot of medieval buildings?
5 is a religious centre?
6 is also an industrial city?
7 is a cultural centre?
8 is an ancient monument, whose function is not completely understood?
9 is a spa town?

3 CD 4.10 Listen and match extracts 1–5 with situations a–e.

a Asking for directions   b In a taxi
c On a guided tour   d A station announcement
e In a hotel reception

4 CD 4.10 Listen again and decide which places from Exercise 1 the couple are visiting in each situation.

1 _____ 2 _____ 3 _____
4 _____ 5 _____

5 Crossing Cultures. Work in groups and follow the instructions. Use the ideas below to help you.

• Choose a tourist destination in your country.
• Write a short guidebook entry for the place. Use the phrases below and in Exercise 1 to help you.
• Don't mention the name of the place in your description!
• Swap your descriptions with another group. Can you guess which place they are describing?

… is a university/industrial city in northwest/southeast/central … .
The centre is full of parks/museums/historic buildings/narrow streets.
It is especially famous for its cathedral/castle/museum/theatre/nightlife.
The church/university/castle/palace dates from the …th century.
A street market/music festival/competition/concert/parade is held here every year.
Millions of tourists come here every year to see … .

Student Activities

Unit 4, Reading and Vocabulary, Exercise 1, page 35.

Check your answers to the Sleep Facts questions on page 34.

1 False. Teenagers need more sleep than adults. Experts believe that teenagers need nine to nine and a half hours a night but most adults only need seven to eight.
2 True
3 True, but there is a big difference in how much animals sleep. Many birds sleep for only two hours a night but koala bears and some cats sleep for sixteen hours!
4 False. When you sleep for 8 hours you use about 520 calories – the same amount your body needs to run for 55 minutes. So, don't forget to eat breakfast!

Unit 4, Reading and Vocabulary, Exercise 6, page 35.

Look at the photo and answer the questions on page 35.

Unit 5, Vocabulary, Exercises 4 and 5, page 47.

CD 24 Read the text and choose the correct words. Then listen and check. What kind of room is the person describing?

I really love this room – it's very bright and ¹ *cosy / uncomfortable*. It's ² *downstairs / upstairs* on the first floor. You get a wonderful view of the trees in the back garden from the window. There's a big ³ *skylight / attic* too, so you get a lot of sunshine in here in the mornings which I love. It's not very ⁴ *roomy / tiny* but I think it's big enough for one person. It can be rather cold in winter, so I have to turn on the ⁵ *freezer / heater* sometimes.

I like the decoration; it's quite tasteful. There are a lot of colourful posters on the ⁶ *floor / door* and an ⁷ *ugly / attractive* old Indian rug. There's a lamp in the corner, a large desk where I keep my computer and printer and a ⁸ *chest of drawers / bookshelf* for my books. I keep all my CDs and records and I have my DVD player in here as well. There's a comfortable old ⁹ *armchair / statue* too. Sometimes I sit and listen to music in the evenings, especially when my girlfriend goes to bed early. But most of the time I work in here. I'm finishing my studies so I've got a lot of work to do. I used to just work in the bedroom but we decided it was better to have another room where I could work in peace.

Unit 5, Speaking, Exercise 3, page 48.

Read the description and answer the questions on page 48.

The picture shows a street of terraced houses in a city. I don't know where it is exactly. Perhaps it's in Germany but it's probably in Britain or Ireland somewhere. The houses are quite small and they haven't got front gardens. But some of the houses look very colourful. In the foreground there are some young kids who are playing football in the street. And there are two old men on the right who are chatting to each other in front of one of the houses. Perhaps they're gossiping about the neighbours! Oh, and there's someone washing his car in the background. It's not a very beautiful street but the atmosphere seems very friendly and relaxed.

Unit 8, Grammar and Reading, Exercise 3, page 68.

Check your scores. Then compare your results with a partner.

Points
1 A 50   B 5
2 A 10   B 25
3 A 20   B 10
4 A 20   B 10
5 A 5   B 40
6 A 10   B 25
7 A 5   B 50
8 A 30   B 5

Results

Points	Ideal jobs
60–90	librarian, therapist, priest, accountant, scientist, nurse
91–120	engineer, computer programmer, pilot, police officer, doctor, architect
121–150	psychologist, writer, translator, fashion designer, teacher, musician
151–180	businessman/woman, lawyer, judge, salesperson, insurance agent, marketing manager
181–210	company director, banker, politician, TV presenter, reporter, actor

Unit 11, Grammar and Reading, Exercise 7, page 97.

Look at the pictures of Kay's flat and answer the questions on page 97.

Unit 12, Writing, Exercise 5, page 110.

Check your answers to questions 1–5 in Exercise 7 on page 110.

1 See you outside theatre at 8 o'clock.
2 Going to club tonight. Want to come?
3 Going home on Friday?
4 Fancy playing football tomorrow?
5 Arriving at station at half six. Wait under clock.

Unit 12, Writing, Exercise 8, page 111.

Check your answers to Exercise 8 on page 111.

Pete

Meeting my cousin on Saturday evening
so can't go.
Want to meet for coffee on Sunday at 3?
Will be upstairs in Toni's – non-smoking area.
Let me know if you can't come.

Vicky XXX

Unit 14, Grammar and Listening, Exercise 3, page 122.

Check Kieran and Becky's answers to the quiz on page 122.

1 Wrong. There are only twelve stars on the EU flag.
2 Correct   3 Correct
4 Wrong. The main meetings are in Strasbourg.
5 Correct

Unit 14, Grammar and Listening, Exercise 8, page 123.

Check your answers to the questions on page 123.

1 Switzerland isn't a member of the EU.
2 Correct
3 There are a hundred cents in one euro.
4 EU citizens are allowed to work and study in other EU countries.
5 Correct   6 Correct
7 The euro hasn't become the official currency in the UK.

Student A activities

Unit 7, Listening, Exercise 8, page 67.

Student A
Look at the predictions and decide if any of them might come true in your country in the next thirty years. Then discuss your ideas with your partner. Use the Speak Out on page 63 to help you.

- A film/pop/sports star will become your country's leader.
- The school-leaving examination will become more difficult.
- People will stop eating traditional national dishes.
- More people will move from the country to the cities.

Perhaps a film star will become our country's president in the future.

Unit 12, Speaking and Listening, Exercise 6, page 107.

Student A

You can't stand The Disaster Channel. You like:
- soap operas, especially *Love and Trust*.
- comedies.
- any programmes with animals in them.

Unit 14, Speaking and Listening, Exercise 6, page 127.

Student A
Follow the instructions. Use Speak Out to help you.

You're travelling across Europe by train (you're on a train from Amsterdam to Prague at the moment). There's somebody else in the compartment who is your age and you decide to start a conversation.
- Ask him/her where he/she is going to and what he/she plans to do for the next few months.
- Your plans for the near future – you're going to visit Prague and Cracow, then study French at Bordeaux University in France.
- Ask and tell each other about your goals in the long term – you want to work as a translator in Belgium or Luxembourg.

Student B activities

Unit 2, Speaking, Exercise 8, page 19.

Student B
Look at text 1 in Exercise 1. Use Speak Out **to roleplay a situation.**

You are the team leader for the Go-Getters working holiday in Scotland.
• The dates of the holiday are 19 July–26 August.
• The accommodation is in a beautiful old castle by a lake.
• There are trains from London to Edinburgh.

You want to know:
• where the caller comes from.
• the age of the caller.
• when the caller can start work.

Unit 7, Listening, Exercise 8, page 67.

Student B
Look at the predictions and decide if any of them might come true in your country in the next thirty years. Then discuss your ideas with your partner. Use the Speak Out **on page 63 to help you.**

• More people will choose to live or work abroad.
• People won't live in blocks of flats any more.
• More English words will enter the language.
• The government will prohibit ultra-realistic computer games.

More people will probably decide to live abroad in the future.

Unit 8, Speaking and Listening, Exercise 8, page 73.

Student B
Your name is Luca/Lucia Toni. You are Marco's flatmate. Someone calls him, but he's not in.

• Say that Marco's not in at the moment.
• Ask him/her if he/she wants to leave a message.
• Ask him/her to spell his/her name and note down his/her email address and phone number.
• Say you will pass on the message.
• Write the message and show it to your partner.

Unit 11, Speaking and Writing, Exercise 5, page 103.

Student B
Read the information and start the conversation.

Your friend is looking very unhappy.
• Ask him/her what has happened.
• Tell your friend not to worry. Perhaps he/she has left it at home.
• Reassure your friend. Suggest that he/she writes a notice and puts it up in the school entrance.

Unit 12, Speaking and Listening, Exercise 6, page 107.

Student B

You really hate soap operas. You love:
• any programme that shows disasters, accidents and catastrophes.
• comedies.
• any programme presented by Wayne Dylan, your favourite TV presenter.

Unit 13, Speaking and Writing, Exercise 6, page 121.

Student B
Read the information and start the conversation.

Your friend asks you for some advice. Listen and make some suggestions.
You also have a problem – you're feeling very stressed because you are studying for exams and you find it difficult to relax. Explain your problem to your friend and:
• ask him/her for some advice.
• thank your friend for his/her advice and tell him/her what you have decided to do.

Unit 14, Speaking and Listening, Exercise 6, page 127.

Student B
Follow the instructions. Use Speak Out **to help you.**

You're travelling to Berlin by train. Another traveller who is your age starts a conversation with you.
• Tell him/her about your plans for the near future – you're going to spend a month with some friends in Berlin, then finish your medical studies in Dublin.
• Ask him/her where he/she is going and what he/she plans to do in the next few months.
• Ask and tell each other about your goals in the long term – you want to work as a doctor for the Red Cross and see the world at the same time.

Student C activity

Unit 12, Speaking and Listening, Exercise 6, page 107.

Student C

You really hate comedies, but you love:
• the latest films.
• programmes on The Disaster Channel.
• the pop star Cherie and watch any programme she appears on.

Student D activity

Unit 12, Speaking and Listening, Exercise 6, page 107.

Student D

You really dislike the film critic, Marcella Brown but you love:
• comedies
• soap operas
• any programme that shows your home town, Otswell.

Irregular verbs

Verb	Past Simple	Past Participle
be	was/were	been
beat	beat	beaten
become	became	become
begin	began	begun
break	broke	broken
bring	brought	brought
broadcast	broadcast	broadcast
build	built	built
buy	bought	bought
can	could	been able
catch	caught	caught
choose	chose	chosen
come	came	come
cost	cost	cost
cut	cut	cut
do	did	done
draw	drew	drawn
dream	dream/dreamt	dreamed/dreamt
drink	drank	drunk
drive	drove	driven
eat	ate	eaten
fall	fell	fallen
feed	fed	fed
feel	felt	felt
fight	fought	fought
find	found	found
flee	fled	fled
fly	flew	flown
forget	forgot	forgotten
get	got	got
give	gave	given
go	went	gone/been
grow	grew	grown
have	had	had
hear	heard	heard
hide	hid	hidden
hit	hit	hit
hold	held	held
keep	kept	kept
know	knew	known
lead	led	led
learn	learned/learnt	learned/learnt
leave	left	left
lend	lent	lent

Verb	Past Simple	Past Participle
let	let	let
lie	lay	lain
light	lit	lit
lose	lost	lost
make	made	made
mean	meant	meant
meet	met	met
misunderstand	misunderstood	misunderstood
pay	paid	paid
put	put	put
read /ri:d/	read /red/	read /red/
ride	rode	ridden
ring	rang	rung
rise	rose	risen
run	ran	run
say	said	said
see	saw	seen
sell	sold	sold
send	sent	sent
set	set	set
shoot	shot	shot
show	showed	shown
sing	sang	sung
sink	sank	sunk
sit	sat	sat
sleep	slept	slept
speak	spoke	spoken
spell	spelled/spelt	spelled/spelt
spend	spent	spent
split	split	split
stand	stood	stood
steal	stole	stolen
swear	swore	sworn
swim	swam	swum
take	took	taken
teach	taught	taught
tell	told	told
think	thought	thought
throw	threw	thrown
understand	understood	understood
wake	woke	woken
wear	wore	worn
win	won	won
write	wrote	written

Pronunciation table

CONSONANTS

Symbol	Key word	Other common spellings
/p/	**p**ark	ha**pp**y
/b/	**b**ath	ru**bb**ish
/t/	**t**ie	bu**tt**er walk**ed**
/d/	**d**ie	te**dd**y bear
/k/	**c**at	**k**ey s**ch**ool che**ck**
/g/	**g**ive	**gh**ost bi**gg**er
/tʃ/	**ch**air	ma**tch** na**t**ural
/dʒ/	**j**eans	a**ge** ga**dg**et sol**di**er
/f/	**f**ace	co**ff**ee **ph**one lau**gh**
/v/	**v**isit	o**f**
/θ/	**th**row	
/ð/	**th**ey	
/s/	**s**ell	**c**inema li**s**ten **ps**ychology **sc**enery me**ss**age
/z/	**z**oo	no**s**e bu**zz**
/ʃ/	**sh**op	**s**ure ambi**ti**on
/ʒ/	mea**s**ure	revi**si**on
/h/	**h**ot	**wh**o
/m/	**m**ap	su**mm**er
/n/	**n**ot	**kn**ow su**nn**y
/ŋ/	si**ng**	thi**n**k
/l/	**l**ot	ba**ll**
/r/	**r**oad	so**rr**y **wr**ite
/j/	**y**ellow	**u**sually **Eu**rope be**au**tiful n**ew**
/w/	**w**arm	**o**ne **wh**ale q**u**ick

VOWELS

Symbol	Key word	Other common spellings
Long and short vowels		
/iː/	f**ee**t	n**ie**ce r**ea**d th**e**se k**ey** rec**ei**pt pol**i**ce
/ɪ/	f**i**t	g**y**m g**ui**tar pr**e**tty
/i/	happ**y**	spaghett**i** marri**ed**
/e/	b**e**d	an**y** br**ea**d fri**e**nd
/æ/	b**a**d	
/ɑː/	b**a**th	**ar**t h**al**f **au**nt h**ear**t
/ɒ/	b**o**ttle	w**a**tch
/ɔː/	b**ough**t	sp**or**t y**our** d**augh**ter sm**al**l dr**aw** w**ar** fl**oor**
/ʊ/	p**u**t	b**oo**k c**oul**d
/uː/	b**oo**t	r**u**de bl**ue** fr**ui**t m**o**ve sh**oe** gr**ou**p fl**ew**
/ʌ/	b**u**t	s**o**me c**ou**sin
/ɜː/	b**ir**d	s**er**ve **ear**ly t**ur**n
/ə/	broth**er**	**the** **a**bout act**or** col**our**
Diphthongs (two vowel sounds pronounced as one)		
/eɪ/	gr**ey**	l**a**ke w**ai**t pl**ay** **eigh**t br**ea**k
/əʊ/	g**o**ld	sh**ow** c**oa**t
/aɪ/	b**y**	l**i**ke d**ie** h**igh** h**eigh**t **eye**s b**uy**
/aʊ/	br**ow**n	ab**ou**t
/ɔɪ/	b**oy**	n**oi**sy
/ɪə/	h**ear**	h**ere** b**eer**
/eə/	h**air**	th**ere** th**eir** squ**are** teddy b**ear**
/ʊə/	s**ure**	p**oor** t**our**
Triphthongs (three vowel sounds pronounced as one)		
/eɪə/	pl**aye**r	
/əʊə/	l**owe**r	
/aɪə/	t**ire**d	
/aʊə/	fl**owe**r	